Creating Your Own
JAPANESE
GARDEN

Creating Your Own
JAPANESE GARDEN

Takashi Sawano

Shufunotomo / Japan Publications

ACKNOWLEDGMENTS

I would like to take this opportunity to thank all the people who helped with the creation and production of this book. I would like to offer particular thanks to the following people at Shufunotomo Co., Ltd. for all of their exceptional patience, professionalism and hard work—Ms. Catherine Meech, Ms. Kate Gorringe-Smith, Ms. Yumi Nakada, Mr. Hidetoshi Nakajima and especially Mr. Shunichi Kamiya, for his encouragement and confidence. Also, I would like to thank Ms. Elizabeth Palmer, who helped me with the first draft. But finally, I would like to offer thanks to my wife, Angela Sawano. Her love, wisdom and strength have inspired me to be the best that I can be.

First Printing, 1999

©Copyright in Japan 1999 by Takashi Sawano
Photographs by Takashi Sawano
Front cover and back cover photographs by Shu Tomioka
Photograph on title page by Katsuhiko Mizuno
Additional photographs by Chihoko Tanefusa and Ryōji Funakoshi
Illustrations by Hidetoshi Nakajima
Book design by Yasuo Fukuda

Published by SHUFUNOTOMO CO., LTD.
2-9, Kanda-Surugadai, Chiyoda-ku, Tokyo, 101-8911 Japan

DISTRIBUTORS
United States: Kodansha America, Inc., through Oxford University Press,
199 Madison Avenue, New York, NY 10016.
Canada: Fitzhenry & Whiteside Ltd.,
195 Allstate Parkway, Markham, Ontario L3R 4T8.
United Kingdom and Europe: Premier Book Marketing Ltd.,
1 Gower Street, London WC1E 6HA.
Australia and New Zealand: Bookwise International,
54 Crittenden Road, Findon, South Australia 5023.
The Far East and Japan: Japan Publications Trading Co., Ltd.,
1-2-1, Sarugaku-cho, Chiyoda-ku, Tokyo 101-0064, Japan

ISBN: 0-87040-962-X
Printed in Hong Kong

PREFACE

In recent years, Japanese gardens have been the subject of a worldwide surge of interest and popularity. Suddenly more and more people want to create Japanese gardens within the framework of their existing gardens. This is partly due to an increasing interest in all types and aspects of Japanese culture; the arts of ikebana, judo, karate, and bonsai, to name a few, are already well established in the West. Perhaps the increasing pressures of our daily lives is also drawing people to seek the peace and serenity which flow from Japanese gardens.

Many books on Japanese gardens can be found in bookstores and libraries, but most do not take into account the different environments found outside Japan nor the diverse materials available worldwide. They tend either to be translations of books written by Japanese landscape architects and gardeners living and working in Japan, or books written by those who visit Japan to research the gardens, with the intention of introducing them to the rest of the world. The illustrations in these books are usually famous old Japanese gardens in Japan. These books are ideal for learning about the history and appearance of Japanese gardens, but lack the practical advice necessary for constructing your own garden.

This book is for those of you who are thinking of designing and making your own Japanese garden, or of hiring a contractor to create one for you. I will show you, step by step, how to accomplish this ideal, utilizing your own special environment and using materials which are readily available. Once finished, your Japanese garden will look as if it is an extension of nature rather than a piece of "Old Japan" transposed onto foreign soil.

My first piece of advice comes from the heart: to make any garden you must love and appreciate nature, for without this your garden will be soulless. Secondly, when making a Japanese garden, you should have an appreciation for, and be able to identify with, Japanese culture and art, otherwise your garden will lack life and spirit; it will simply be a regular garden that happens to contain some Japanese artifacts. If you already have such an understanding, you are halfway to creating your Japanese garden, or, as the Japanese saying goes, "you have already bought the ticket for the train." Without this understanding you won't even get as far as the station. Before you begin, I therefore strongly encourage you to spend some time learning about Japan and gaining some understanding of other Japanese arts in order to imbue your garden with a Japanese soul. You can do this by reading, visiting museums and exhibitions on Japanese art, or watching Japanese movies.

I came to England in 1974, and have since made my home here. During this time I have designed and made many Japanese gardens, from small private gardens to large public spaces of over two acres. It is from this direct experience that I have drawn the material for my book. I am sure you'll find the step-by-step instructions easy to follow, and I have also included many drawings and photographs to illustrate the points I make. All of the gardens featured were made outside Japan.

I believe that as the interest in and understanding of Japanese culture continues to spread, so will the popularity of and desire for Japanese gardens.

I hope that this book will give pleasure to all those of you who, like me, are captivated by the gardens of Japan, and that it will help you to create a garden of your own that you can enjoy day after day.

Takashi Sawano

CONTENTS

1 | WHAT IS A JAPANESE GARDEN?

The differences between Japanese and Western gardens are as vast as the differences between the two cultures. Perhaps the most fundamental difference is that the Japanese garden is intended to be a microcosm of nature, while Western gardens often tend to serve a utilitarian purpose.

Another striking difference lies in the use of color and shape. In a Japanese garden, the main color focus is green, with trees and shrubs providing a subtle variety of shades. There are few annual flowers and bulbs; flowers are generally limited to the blossoms of flowering trees and shrubs, such as cherry and camellia. Color may be used in a solid block, such as a bed of azalea, but is never intermingled with other colors, as it might be in a Western herbaceous border.

Western gardens often display large trees in their natural shapes alongside smaller shrubs and trees that have been trimmed into geometric and artificial shapes. Japanese gardeners, however, trim and train their plants and trees into what may be termed a "stylized naturalism," which is an attempt to capture the pure and essential shape of the plant. This is perhaps best exemplified by the elegant and angular pines associated with Japanese gardens. The very first instruction in the 11th-century *Sakuteiki* ("Treatise on Garden Making") is to observe and learn from nature. The idea is not simply to transpose a view that you have seen—that is merely imitation—but to absorb the atmosphere and feeling, and to use your own ideas and imagination to recreate the same mood in your garden.

An aspect of Japanese gardens that can be unsettling at first to those who are not familiar with them, is their asymmetry. While Western gardens tend to employ a 50%:50% symmetrical balance with a central focus point, Japanese gardens have a balance of either 60%:40% or 70%:30%; the focal point is never in the center of the garden.

Opposite: The famous garden at Sanzen'in, Kyoto

Below: Dry garden and grove of trees seen through the window of Ginkakuji, the Silver Pavilion, Kyoto

Water, stone, and garden ornaments are used as features in both Western and Japanese gardens, but to different effect. Western gardens may feature ornate benches, fountains and pergolas which are placed to stand out against the natural backdrop, while Japanese gardens contain rustic stone lanterns, water basins and bamboo fences which blend with their natural surroundings.

THE HISTORICAL BACKGROUND

Origins

It is thought that many of the ideas that have come to be the basic precepts for constructing Japanese gardens originated in China. These ideas probably arrived in Japan with the Chinese and Korean priests, scribes, potters and weavers who imparted their knowledge of Confucianism and Buddhism, Chinese writing, political administration, as well as their technical skills to the Imperial Court in the sixth century.

The earliest known reference to Japanese gardens appears in the *Nihonshoki* ("Chronicle of Japan"), which dates from the sixth century and is the first recorded book on Japanese art and culture. Many of the observations made in regard to gardening are just as valid today.

Indeed, many texts from the earliest days are still relevant today. For example the *Sakuteiki* remains the bible for Japanese garden designers. This book clearly and concisely reveals the basic ideas that lie not only behind Japanese gardens, but behind all Japanese art and culture. The main subject of the book is stone—a vital element in a Japanese garden. The importance of this work in both the development of Japanese gardens through history and in their creation today cannot be overemphasized.

Kyoto

Kyoto was the capital city during the Heian period (794-1185) and proved to have the ideal environment and conditions for creating gardens with beautiful natural landscapes and an abundance of rock, mountains and natural streams. What's more, the long period of peace which spanned the decades of Kyoto's reign allowed the arts to flourish amidst an influx of cultural borrowing from China.

Above: A garden landscape with pond, Jōruriji, Kyoto
Below: A three-story pagoda facing a pond, Jōruriji, Kyoto

A typical Zen contemplative garden, consisting mainly of rock and stone

During this period, gardeners moved away from merely reproducing the popular Chinese gardens of the T'ang dynasty, to using traditional Chinese techniques to design gardens suited to Japanese tastes and habitats. Plants, grasses and trees were transplanted from their natural habitat, and gardens resembling rich and colorful paintings were created. The Heian-era gardens of Byōdōin, Jōruriji and Mōtsuji temples can still be seen today. When they were built, however, these gardens could only be enjoyed by the nobility.

Zen

Zen Buddhism was introduced to Japan from China during the Kamakura period (1185-1333), but its profound effect upon all Japanese art and culture was not felt until the Muromachi period (1336-1573). The Zen priests became powerful and respected teachers and advisors to the court and government. As garden designers, they moved towards a more simple and symbolic style, imbued with philosophical meaning. The simplicity of the Chinese *sumi* ink painting style was frequently represented in gardens and the gardens often contained no plants, just stone and sand.

Hideyoshi Toyotomi

In the Azuchi-Momoyama period (1573-1598), Japan became a unified country under the leadership of the shogun Hideyoshi Toyotomi. The shogun's lavish personal tastes affected the entire nation's art and culture. He built many large and impressive castles and the elaborate gardens reflected this grandeur. He also introduced unusual tropical plants such as *Cycas revoluta*. However, tastes soon began to revert from the rich and exaggerated back to the rustic and simple.

Above: The elegant contours of the Byōdōin, Kyoto, were inspired by the shape of a phoenix about to take flight
Below: Another view of the Byōdōin showing the dry garden between the temple and the lake

Cycas revoluta to the right of the stone lantern

11

Teahouses

It was during the Azuchi-Momoyama period that the teahouse, with its surrounding tea garden, was introduced to Japan. It was also during Hideyoshi Toyotomi's rule that the decorative simplicity of stepping stones, stone lanterns and water basins was introduced into gardens from temples. Japanese gardens were no longer enjoyed only by the aristocracy and ruling class, as their popularity had spread to the new middle class of merchants.

Most of the old gardens that are admired today by visitors to Japan were created during this period. Musō Kokushi, one of the most famous garden designers of his era, was also a famous Zen priest. His gardens of Tenryūji, Kinkakuji, Daitokuji and Ryōanji are still in existence today. Two famous tea masters who were also renowned for their gardens during this period were Sen no Rikyū and Furuta Oribe, and their gardens at Sanpōin and Nishihonganji can also be seen today.

Above: The Golden Pavilion, Kinkakuji, Kyoto
Below: Rocks arranged around the pond at Tenryūji, Kyoto

Edo—The New Capital

The Edo period (1603-1867) signifies the move of Japan's capital to Edo, today's Tokyo. The popularity of the tea ceremony had spread, and many tea gardens were constructed during this time. In addition, both private and public gardens flourished, and laymen began to design their own gardens. Layouts became more relaxed, and individual tastes were taken into consideration. For example, if the owner liked flowers he might transplant wild flowers, or if fish were an interest, the pond might be well stocked with *koi* (carp).

Colorful *koi* swimming in a pond: an image often associated with Japanese gardens

Paradoxically, this period also saw the establishment of formal styles of garden design, an indication that gardens had come into their own as an art form. The *Shin* style, which is the most refined, has very strict rules, the *So* style is relatively casual and free from rules, while the *Gyō* style is between the two. These classifications originally referred to calligraphy, but are now used to encompass all forms of artistic expression. One of the most eminent designers during this period was Kobori Enshū, whose famous gardens include Katsura Rikyū, Shugakuin and Kōrakuen.

Above: Trimmed bushes representing stones, Koishikawa Kōrakuen, Tokyo
Center: A pond and a bridge, seen from a distance, Koishikawa Kōrakuen, Tokyo
Below: An *azumaya* (summer house) quietly faces the landscape, Katsura Rikyū, Kyoto

13

Foreign Influences

The Meiji and Taishō periods (1868-1912 and 1912-1926, respectively) saw the opening of the country to foreign influence beyond that of China and Korea, and many new ideas and materials were introduced into Japanese gardens. The creation of Western-style areas within an existing Japanese garden became popular. Prefectures began to establish departments for the environment as interest grew in public parks and playgrounds, and to realise the need to conserve areas of land as parks or "green" areas which would be preserved from development.

Japanese Gardens Abroad

Conversely, at this time Japan was also having a considerable influence on other countries. After Japan was opened in 1868, many wealthy foreigners visited and were captivated by the peaceful and beautiful gardens they found there. They returned to their homelands not only with dreams of Japanese gardens but sometimes with the Japanese gardeners who could recreate those dreams in new surroundings. Many of them imported ornaments and plants from Japan. They then transformed a section of their garden into a replica of a traditional Japanese garden or of a scene remembered from their travels. Many such gardens still exist, albeit often in disrepair.

The twentieth century has seen the popularity and appreciation of the Japanese garden spread worldwide. Landscape architects now create gardens in settings as diverse as offices, museums, public parks and exhibition spaces, as well as in private houses and apartments.

Above: The English skyline is thrown into contrast against this traditional Japanese garden, Kyoto Garden, Holland Park, England
Above-center: A dry garden filled with an array of interesting rocks, Tenshin-en, Museum of Fine Arts, U.S.A.
Below-center: Stepping stones on a pond, the Japanese garden at Jardin Albert Kahn, France
Below: An *azumaya* (summer house) with a thatched roof overlooks the Japanese garden, Heale House, England

14

Above: A still pond, Jardin Albert Kahn, France
Center: A *yukimi* lantern on a small island, Pool, Compton, England
Below: A wooden gate resembling a Japanese *torii* gate, Tenshin-en, Museum of Fine Arts, Boston, U.S.A.

In and *Yō* symbol

In: Black
Yō: White

JAPANESE AESTHETICS

In creating any kind of garden, but especially a Japanese garden, it is possible—with just one tree or rock—to recreate a particular image or scene from nature. In such a concentrated area the seasons or the elements can be seen and appreciated to a greater extent than in the actual environment. In the smaller space everything is both magnified and condensed.

To evoke the desired feeling, neither financial considerations nor the size of the land available are crucial issues. What is important is that you are familiar with certain Japanese aesthetic concepts before you begin to consider the details of your garden. It is common knowledge that in order to transpose the art of one culture upon another and to achieve a harmonious unity, a knowledge and appreciation of both is important. Following are some of the fundamental concepts which lie behind Japanese garden design.

In and *Yō*
To the Japanese, the world is a scale balanced by the presence of two opposing elements called *in* and *yō*. This concept originally came from China where it is called *ying* and *yang*. Everything in the world can be seen as an expression of one or the other. For example, evening is *in* or *ying*; day is *yō* or *yang*. Female is *in*; male is *yō*. Winter is *in*; summer is *yō*. Even though they are opposite in concept and meaning, they complement each other and thus create balance in the universe. The concept of *in* and *yō* is present in all aspects of a Japanese garden. For example, stone is *in* and water is *yō*; deciduous trees are *in* and evergreens are *yō*.

Imagine a situation where there is no distinction between day and night. If there were only darkness or light there would be no rejuvenation period for plants, animals or humans. The balance between *in* and *yō* is crucial.

15

In Western thought, balance is achieved when weight is distributed evenly: 50:50. But, to the Oriental mind, as long as the the sum of the parts adds up to 100 percent, the scale is balanced; a ratio of 70:30 or 90:10 is acceptable—even preferable.

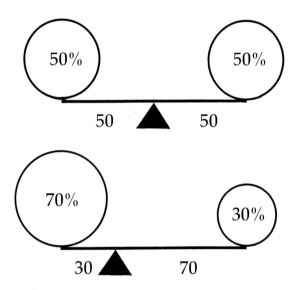

This acceptance of asymmetrical balance lies at the foundation of all Japanese thought, art and culture. To the Western eye, when confronted for the first time by the asymmetrical nature of a Japanese garden, may find its effect somewhat unsettling. When you design your garden, the concept of *in* and *yō* must be taken into account along with the idea of asymmetrical balance. You might consider letting 70 percent represent land and 30 percent be water, or use 60 percent trees and 40 percent flowering material.

Shibumi

This word conjures up an idea of gentle but continuous motion, almost like drifting or floating in a mist free from shocks or sudden changes.

As early as the seventh century, the Japanese began to transplant trees and grass from the wild into their gardens to recreate and enjoy the feeling of "nature in the wild." You can even create this kind of atmosphere in a very small area. In fact, a small space is easier. Just imagine two or three stems of a sensitive, small-leafed variety of bamboo surrounded by an area of grey pebbles, in an otherwise empty scene. This insignificant offering of bamboo can suggest a vast bamboo grove swaying and bending in the wind.

A bamboo grove is suggested here by a few stems of bamboo in a landscape otherwise void of living materials

Yūgen

This concept suggests the feeling of an enveloping presence which is eclipsing or sheltering a thing of immense beauty. Beauty is merely suggested rather than made obvious. This same feeling exists in the art of Japanese lacquer, *urushi*, where layers of brilliant and shining lacquer are applied to an object. Finally, a matt finish is applied to the surface. If the artist had just applied a layer of matt paint from the outset, you would not sense the beautiful and sumptuous lacquer glowing richly beneath its dull covering.

Yūgen is an essential mood in the Japanese garden. For example, although a garden may have a waterfall, stone lantern or pagoda as its focal point, this may be partially obscured by carefully placed shrubs or plants. Thus the essence of the object is glimpsed or sensed through its green covering.

The stand of this lantern has been purposely hidden from view

Yūgen can also be represented in the way the roots of some trees partially grow above soil level. This suggests the enormity and depth of the root system deep in the earth.

The turbulence created by water splashing against and churning around a large stone set in the center of a stream creates the impression of a strong and fast current, even though such a current does not actually exist.

A *yukimi* lantern partially hidden from view reflects the mood of *yūgen*

Large stones placed in the middle of a pond represent islands on a sea of waves

17

Shakkei

Also referred to as "borrowed scenery," *shakkei* is an old, important and much used technique in the art of Japanese gardening. It is used to incorporate surrounding scenery into the overall view to make the garden appear to extend beyond its boundaries. *Shakkei* does not mean copying the external view, but planning your garden with this view in mind, so that it becomes an extension of your garden. Examples of this technique can be seen in many old Japanese gardens which are open to the public. If you have a grove of trees outside the boundaries of your garden, try to create a scene where these distant trees look as if they are actually a part of your garden. This technique is difficult to employ in the Japanese gardens of the West, as in most instances the surrounding scenery will conflict rather than blend harmoniously with the garden.

The shape of the trimmed shrubs and trees blends well with the soft lines of the mountains and hills in the background

Wabi

This concept, whereby an old object or artifact which has been cherished and enjoyed over the years is valued because it radiates a feeling of age and history, originated with the tea ceremony.

In terms of a Japanese garden, an old, weathered stone water basin will help to conjure up the image of pure water tumbling over ancient stones in the center

of the city. In order to imbue your garden with a sense of *wabi*, choose pieces of stone which are old and mossy or set a stone lantern in a simple style such as *ikekomi*, which means a portion of its base is hidden by gravel or sand.

Above: Stones covered in moss add a sense of *wabi* to a garden
Below: Timeworn artifacts, such as this metal lantern, are preferred over new ones

Above: A moss-covered bridge blends well with the surrounding greenery and pond.
Below: An *ikekomi* lantern with part of its base buried below the soil

Items such as bamboo fences, bridges and stone should have a mature, weathered quality rather than a bright new shine. Use subtle shades of evergreens rather than brilliant verdant colors, choose varieties of plants, grasses or weeds that grow naturally in the wild, such as *Cryptomeria japonica* (*sugi*), *Chamaecpraris obtusa* (*hinoki*), *Ardisia crenata* (*manryō*), or *Juncus effusus* (*tokusa*).

Try to create in your Japanese garden the feeling that it has been tenderly cherished and nurtured for one hundred years, and that you are simply carrying on the tradition. It should have the feeling of a carefully cultivated agedness. My favorite simile is the idea of a man who in his youth was full of energy and adventure, trying anything and everything. In old age the same man still enjoys life, perhaps to an even greater extent, but in a simple, refined way, and with a lifetime of experience within him.

THE ELEMENTS OF A JAPANESE GARDEN

While many of the elements employed in the Japanese garden can also be found in the gardens of the West, the difference lies in the overall effect that they are used to create.

While Western gardeners seek to use elements to accessorize or catch the eye, the Japanese gardener strives to reflect the inherent characteristics of the elements it uses, and it is this which gives Japanese gardens their special quality of nature untouched by man.

WATER

One of the most important elements in a Japanese garden is water. Indeed, it would be difficult to imagine a garden without a pond, stream or lake, or at least the suggestion of water.

Unlike stone and plants, water has no fixed shape of its own, taking the shape of its container whether it be a vase, water basin or river. It is in constant motion and its shape is ever-changing as it strives to maintain its natural level in relation to the land.

Above: The cascading waterfall does not affect the serenity of the pond
Below: A scene of perfect tranquility, Sarusawaike pond, Kōfukuji, Nara

Historically, the primary consideration when planning a garden in Japan was the availability and situation of the water supply. Only after this was calculated was the layout of the garden planned, as it depended upon the natural flow of water.

The main reason that so many gardens were created in Kyoto, the ancient capital, was because of its abundant natural water supply. The traditional rules laid down for the use of water in Japanese gardens are based upon Kyoto's natural environment. Since it was not always possible to adapt Kyoto garden designs for use in other environments, additional rules were created to take the conditions of other locations into account. Gardeners did not attempt to divert or create a new water supply, but utilized the natural source.

Western gardeners may also include a water section, but their attitudes in regard to its construction are different. Their first consideration is dividing the land into different areas or sections. Only then is the decision made as to where to place the water feature, and then how to bring the water supply to the chosen site. The water is therefore not used in its natural course.

Ponds and Lakes

The most common water element utilized in a Japanese garden is the pond. From ancient times, ponds have featured not only in the gardens of Japan and China, but in Western countries too. They not only create an illusion of width and depth, but also introduce a sense of movement into the environment.

In the famous old Japanese gardens, ponds and lakes were usually based upon natural sea, lake or river scenes. To recreate the natural banks, these ponds were often edged with stone or wood. They were usually fed by a nearby stream or waterfall, and the overflow carried out by a natural stream, thus providing constant ebb and flow.

As garden designers moved away from imitating their natural surroundings and began to use their imaginations to recreate the moods they observed in nature, the pond no longer represented just an image of the sea, but was used to create different scenes or to evoke certain feelings. One side, for example, might contain large, rough stones planted with muscular pine trees to represent a rugged seashore, while another area might have a muddy plain with reeds and rushes to create a contrasting atmosphere.

The pond at the Silver Pavilion, Ginkakuji, Kyoto

Streams and Waterfalls

As in nature, streams and waterfalls add a sense of dynamism to a garden. If you imagine a natural mountain scene where a river flows down through a rugged valley or gorge, this same effect can be achieved in a garden by creating a narrow stream with a layout of large stones on either side. A large stone in the middle of the stream creates both sound and movement as the water splashes against it. Gradually changing the bed of the stream, as it descends, from cobblestones to pebbles to sand makes the water gradually flow more gently and quietly as it reaches the lower level.

Waterfalls may fall in one straight cascading column, creating a very strong atmosphere or a

Water is essential to a Japanese garden

more gentle effect can be created by having the water flow over two or three stones. Sometimes the water can be made to fall away from the rock surface at an angle or be diverted into two or three separate flows.

The sound of this waterfall provides background music for the garden

The Suggestion of Water

In contrast to a gushing waterfall, water may also feature in a garden in a more placid form: a still pool of water in a stone water basin or a quiet, rhythmical drip from a water spout whose source is invisible. Water may not actually be present at all, but merely be symbolized in the raked patterns of a sand "sea" in a dry garden.

STONE

Another vital element in Japanese gardens is stone. While plants and trees change with the seasons and perhaps even die, stone represents unchanging stability.

If you leaf through the ancient *Sakuteiki*, you will see that it is concerned primarily with stone, laying down strict rules for combining and positioning of formations within the garden. Even within stone groupings, there is a harmony between upright and horizontal rocks. In accordance with the Japanese philosophy of *in* and *yō*, the slanting or feminine stone represents *in*, and the upright or masculine type, *yō*.

Stone takes many forms in the Japanese garden, as described below.

Rocks

The rocks used in Japanese gardens are natural shapes created by time and weathering, not cut by man into artificial forms. Rocks also have symbolic meanings; an island in the center of a pond, for example, may represent a crane or a tortoise, the symbols of longevity and happiness.

A large piece of rock molded by time and nature

Cobblestones

These round, smooth stones (approximately 10-30cm in diameter) are quite common in Japanese gardens. They can be used for the bed of a strongly flowing stream, to create a natural seashore scene on the banks of a pond, to build a stone wall, or in the making of stone steps or paths.

Pebbles

Smaller than cobblestones (about 2-5cm in diameter), pebbles are similarly round and smooth. They are often used as the base of a gently flowing river bed. Pebbles can be obtained in such colors as white, black, grey, red and yellow. One of the most popular types is the black, round and shiny *nachiguro*. They are not only used around water but to form a boundary between different materials such as sand and soil.

Gravel

Also referred to as "chips," pieces of gravel are approximately 2cm in diameter, mid-range in size between pebbles and sand. In a dry garden, gravel can be raked into various designs to represent a calm or a rough sea, depending on the mood you wish to create.

When raked into different patterns, gravel can create the effect of a sea in motion

Sand

Sand refers to very small particles of stone which have the consistency of sugar. It is used in a variety of different ways and, as with chips, can be raked into different patterns. It is best used in an interior environment, as wind can be a problem outside.

ORNAMENTS

The ornaments associated with Japanese gardens originally appeared in gardens created for the tea ceremony. These gardens were designed to complement the simple rustic beauty of the teahouses and therefore the ornaments were also subtle and understated, made from natural elements such as plain stone or wood, and often served practical functions.

Nowadays, these ornaments have mostly lost their functional purposes but are still able to imbue a garden with subtle beauty and tranquility. These man-made objects never clutter a garden or stand out obtrusively but blend in harmoniously with their natural surroundings.

Stone Lanterns (*Tōrō*)

These well-known ornaments originated in China and Korea. From early times in Japan they were given as donations to temples and shrines where they were used to light the way for worshippers at night. By the end of the 14th century they began to be used in Japanese gardens.

There are many different sizes and shapes of lantern. The most popular is the *kasuga*, which has its origins in a religious setting and is tall and strong, creating an imposing presence. Examples can be seen in temples and shrines all over Japan, as well as in parks and private gardens.

The tall *kasuga* lantern

The *yukimi* is used in both large and small gardens and especially near water. *Yukimi* means "snow-viewing lantern," since the roof section is relatively wide and flat and gathers snow in the winter.

The roof of the *yukimi* lantern collects snow during the winter

The curved pedestal gives the *rankei* lantern its unique asymmetrical shape and balance. It is most effective at the edge of a shore leaning over a pond, while its modern appearance makes it a good choice for contemporary garden designs.

The curved *rankei* lantern

The small and roundish *misaki* lantern

The petite *misaki* lantern is often used in smaller gardens. A favorite position is at the end of an island or peninsula where it is surrounded by water on three sides.

Water Basin (*Tsukubai*)

Water basins were originally used for purification purposes at temples, where visitors would rinse their hands and mouth before entering, and also for simple hygiene. By the end of the Azuchi Momoyama period (1568-1600), their use had extended to the tea ceremony and they are now one of the most attractive and popular ornaments in the Japanese garden.

Above: This water basin resembles a pumpkin
Below: A rock with a hole carved in it makes a perfect water basin

Water Pipe (*Kakehi*)

Now used either alone or with the water basin, a water pipe was originally used to transport water from a mountain stream to a garden pond.

Water pipe

Deer Scarer (*Shishi odoshi*)

This is a system by which water is fed through a bamboo pipe and, when the pipe is full, one end falls and strikes a stone set beneath it, making a sharp knocking sound. Its origin was to startle wild animals such as deer, dogs or boar which might enter the garden. Now it is used purely for decorative purposes.

Above: A deer scarer
Below: A deer scarer hidden from view. Only its clicking sound will be heard

Stepping Stones (*Tobi ishi*)

In the old tea gardens, these stones served to lead the visitor on a meandering route through the garden so as to give them time to calm the mind and dispense with worldly thoughts while appreciating the different scenes of nature. Stepping stones were originally designed as a means of walking around the garden in comfort in the same way that western gardens contain paths. But they also had a decorative use and were not arranged in straight lines but in a variety of different patterns which have evolved over the centuries.

Above: Here the stepping stones—islands of dramatic blue in a sea of grey pebbles—create an effect not unlike a modern art installation
Below: Stepping stones across a stream suggest an endless path

Fences (*Kakine*)

The two principal uses of fences are to separate different areas of the garden, or to hide unwanted objects or views. But Japanese fences differ from their Western counterparts in that they do not simply block out the view, but act as a screen through which elements of what lies beyond can be glimpsed. In this way the fence suggests that something lies beyond the line of vision, making the garden appear larger. Rather than a solid brick or wood, fences made from bamboo or other plant materials are used.

A bamboo fence with bamboo twigs

A bamboo sleeve fence (*sodegaki*) is a short fence or screen used to divide two areas or garden scenes. For example, it may be used to separate the dry garden from the water section, or the side entrance from the front of the house. Bamboo is indigenous to Japan and many different varieties are used to make numerous styles of fences.

"Sleeve" fences used as a screen

A living plant fence (*ikegaki*), as the name suggests, is made of living plant material such as camellia, usually the sazanqua variety, or conifer. While waiting for the fence to reach maturity it is usual to erect a simple bamboo fence to support the growing plants.

Above: A living plant fence
Below: A bamboo fence used as a boundary wall

Gates (*Mon*)

These are an important item in Japanese gardens and are made of either bamboo or wood. But, unlike the Western idea of a barrier, gates in a Japanese garden suggest a connection between the different environments on either side. The design is often a simple, open one which can be seen through.

Above: The main gate leading to the front garden
Below: An inner gate in the middle of a tea garden

Bridges (*Hashi*)

When making even a very small island within a pond it is customary to erect a bridge leading from the island to the mainland. Japanese bridges are generally made of wood or stone and should have a gentle arch, unlike the sharp incline of many Chinese-style bridges. Sometimes a bridge can be built for purely ornamental purposes as a point of interest.

Above: Contrasting bridges cross the same pond
Below: Slabs of stone are often used as bridges

Summer House (*Azumaya* or *Machiai*)

A summer house can be erected in a large garden or park, or at a place that offers a special view. It is a small, simple wooden building, open in the front, with four pillars, a plain roof and a bench inside where one may sit and enjoy the scene. Using a summer house in a small area is not recommended as it will make the garden look smaller.

Above: A stone lion guards the entrance to a summer house
Below: An airy summer house with wooden and stone benches

PLANTS

Although some Japanese gardens do not contain any living plants, those that do are carefully planned and balanced. The main color is green, with trees and shrubs providing a subtle variety of shades, with perhaps a splash of color provided by the blossoms of flowering trees and shrubs. They blend harmoniously with the other elements of the garden, the stone, ornaments and water. Ground cover may also be used to soften the effect of the garden.

Plants used may be shrubs or trees, deciduous or coniferous. Often they will be trimmed and shaped into stylized shapes.

The abundant variety of species of shrubs and trees on the market offer a wonderful selection, but rarely will such a variety be found in a single Japanese garden. Below are just some of the most famous and common trees, shrubs and ground cover; many others can be found in Appendix 1.

Trees: Pine (*Matsu*)

From the earliest times, this was considered to be the "king" of garden plants and believed to bring good fortune. In the floral art of ikebana it is used for New Year arrangements as a symbol of good luck. There are many different varieties of pine found worldwide, but the types most often used in Japanese gardens which can be found in many other countries are listed in Appendix 1. The character of each is very different. Black pine, for example, is strong and bold, while white pine has a more gentle and noble air.

Even in Japan the techniques of shaping and trimming vary from one region to another.

The graceful curves of a pine tree in the garden of a private home

The growth of the tree varies according to trimming, environment and climate and there is a marked difference between the northern and southern islands of Japan.

When you see a view of the Japanese coastline with pine trees hanging precariously onto the jagged rock these are usually the black pine. This is also the most common variety of pine to be grown as bonsai.

A group of pine trees adorns a small island

Shrubs: Bamboo (*Take*)

Bamboo has a very fresh and beautiful new green color. It grows perpendicular to the ground and forms natural sections at regular intervals along the stem and the branches. The sound of the wind rustling through the leaves in a bamboo grove has a very tranquil and calming effect and has inspired Japanese poets throughout the ages. This feeling of serenity is closely associated with Japanese gardens.

A serene bamboo grove

Ground cover: Moss (*Koke*)

Ground cover softens the appearance of a Japanese garden. In particular, the Japanese consider it extremely fortunate whenever moss appears in a garden, since it brings a feeling of age and imbues the garden with *wabi* and *yūgen*. Although in many cultures moss is considered to be a weed and is immediately removed, in Japanese gardens it is deliberately cultivated, not only on the ground but also on the surface of stones and stone ornaments.

Above: Soft green moss conceals the ground
Below: A thatched roof covered in moss adds a touch of age and softness to this hut

TRADITIONAL TYPES OF GARDENS

The Japanese garden may be classified as one of three separate styles:
1. *Kaiyūshiki* (Stroll garden)
2. *Karesansui* (Dry garden)
3. *Chaniwa* (Tea garden)

KAIYŪSHIKI

This type of garden is usually quite large. It is a garden that is designed to be walked through, thus allowing one to admire the different scenic areas which gradually unfold as one strolls through it. The focal point is generally a large pond around which different views or scenes of nature are featured. As the visitor strolls through the garden, different landscapes are revealed, such as mountains, waterfalls, streams, islands in the lake, forests and open meadows. The *kaiyūshiki* garden may also incorporate the other types of gardens.

This is the most difficult type of garden to design, even for professionals. It requires clear and concise ideas and thorough planning to create unity among the different views. Due to its size and complexity, it is generally not suitable for a domestic environment and instructions for creating one are therefore not included in this book.

KARESANSUI

This is by far the most distinctive type of Japanese garden, and a great deal of symbolism lies behind it. Although they contained no living materials—such as plants, trees and water—these gardens were designed to represent the mountainous ranges and other natural scenery of Japan. The literal translation of *karesansui*, "not using water," is deceptive as the concept of water is extremely important in the dry garden. Sand or chippings raked into special patterns represent waves, while a large piece of stone or a mound of soil conjures up the image of a mountain or an island. *Karesansui* gardens today may include living materials such as plants and trees but in a limited and controlled way.

Ancient gardens of this type, which were designed by Buddhist monks to suggest the ideals of Zen Buddhism, can still be seen in Japan (e.g. Ginkakuji, Ryōanji, Daisen'in). Zen emphasizes the concept of simplicity in the sense of stripping away the surface layers to reveal the essential truth beneath, as is evident in the simple beauty of the dry garden. This, I believe, is the reason for the rising popularity of the dry garden today, when the pressures of life make it even more important to appreciate and enjoy the feeling of peace and tranquillity which emerge from this type of garden.

Aerial view of a "stroll" garden, Heian jingū, Kyoto

CHANIWA

The original setting for this type of garden was in front of, or surrounding, a teahouse. The tea ceremony was sometimes performed in the evening, so the gardens were lit by candles placed inside stone lanterns. Before entering the teahouse, guests purify both their bodies and minds in order to enter with a pure spirit. Thus a stone water basin was placed just outside to ritually cleanse the hands and mouth. In order to create a barrier between the peaceful tranquillity of the tea garden and the busy life left behind, a bamboo fence or sleeve fence created a symbolic division between the two.

There is a strong connection between the house and tea garden. Like the *kaiyūshiki* garden, it should be very natural but, because of its diminutive size, more simple. It should suggest a large space in just a small area.

A small *chaniwa* (tea garden) viewed from a Japanese-style room

Above: Rock islands amid a sea of pebbles, Ryōanji, Kyoto
Below: A conical mound of sand representing a mountain, Silver Pavilion, Ginkakuji, Kyoto

2 | JAPANESE GARDENS IN WESTERN SETTINGS

If they are designed and created with care, Japanese gardens can blend surprisingly well into Western settings. They may even provide solutions that Western gardens do not offer to problems such as lack of space, insufficient light, even poor soil.

The following pages feature examples of gardens I have designed and constructed based on the *chaniwa* and *karesansui* garden styles. All of the gardens shown were made in the West, using materials that were locally available. You might choose to adapt a design or to combine ideas from two or three examples when you embark on designing your own unique garden.

FRONT GARDENS

When making a front garden, great care must be taken so as not to disrupt the general view of which the garden is merely one part. In order to preserve harmony with your neighborhood–as well as your neighbors–I would suggest that you save the unique, traditional garden designs for the rear of the house, and concentrate on a style that blends well with its surroundings and only suggests a Japanese influence or feeling for the front.

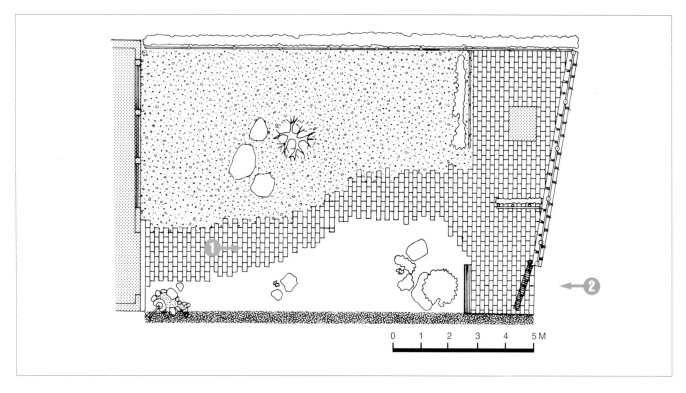

Example 1

This garden is situated in a quiet suburb of London. The client specifically wanted a traditional Japanese garden and I therefore decided to close the garden off from public view. I did so by means of a tall bamboo fence which consists of two separate but overlapping sections. The garden cannot be seen from the street, and the visitor must walk behind the front section of the fence before catching his or her first glimpse of the garden. A granite path curves gracefully around a group of stones and a camellia bush. A flowering cherry tree creates a contrasting focal point while a row of conifers conceals the refuse area.

❶ View from house

❷ View from entrance

Example 2

This is the garden of a seafront island home. The brief from the client requested that the garden be designed to create an illusion of space and to suggest a sea view from the living areas. The original paved garden was interspersed with plant containers. The present owners had extended the front entrance hall making the garden smaller.

The main problem was that the garden was exposed to salty sea spray and to strong winds. I therefore decided to keep the planting to a minimum and to emphasize the water feature. This was done by allowing water containing *koi* to flow from a gully outside the study window into a stone pond in the entrance hall. The water basin was an old trough used to feed pigs which I discovered during a visit to Wales.

A stone lantern is the focal point of the garden and the garage wall is disguised by a bamboo screen fence with an edging of curved roof tiles. The bamboo sleeve fence hides the side passage and acts as a windbreak from the strong sea winds.

❶ View from entrance

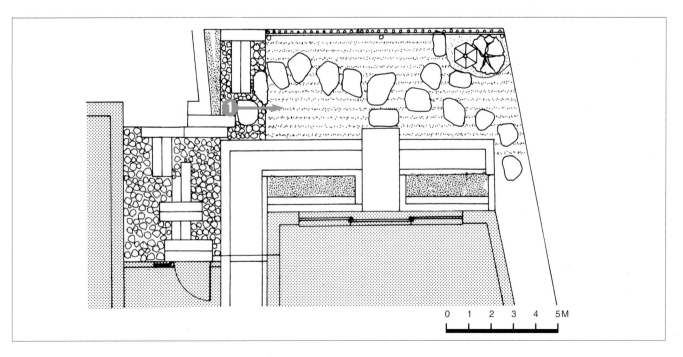

0 1 2 3 4 5M

❶ View from garden

BACK GARDENS

Back gardens allow for greater experimentation than front gardens generally do. Screened from passersby and not required to fit into any neighborhood patterns, the back garden is more suitable than the front for indulging in unusual designs.

However, if necessity dictates that your back garden also function as a social setting, I would strongly recommend that you reserve only a portion of the total garden area for your Japanese garden.

Example 1

The original Japanese garden on this site had been created in the early 20th century. By the time I was approached by the present owners to restore it, the house had changed hands many times and the garden had been sadly neglected and was overgrown.

The brief from my clients expressed a desire to create a garden which provided an open play area for their young children and a large space for their frequent business and social entertaining.

However, they wanted to retain part of the existing Japanese garden. I decided to reserve the central area as a lawn for the play and entertainment areas. This was separated from the Japanese garden by a low bamboo fence. I wanted to restore as much of the original Japanese garden as possible, but this meant cutting, trimming and reshaping about 70 percent of the plants, trees and shrubs.

During my excavations I discovered many varieties of rare plants and some of the original, imported garden ornaments. I also discovered a winding stream to which I added a circulating water system. Only the summer house and stone lantern were new additions. This is a good example of *shakkei* (borrowed scenery), since the garden blends very well with the surrounding woodland and appears larger than its actual size.

0 1 2 3 4 5M

Example 2

The design and creation of this city garden proved for me to be a great adventure. The house had lain empty for a number of years before being purchased by its present owners, who asked me to design a garden utilizing the entire space available. Unfortunately the land sloped sharply downwards, away from the house, making the creation of the garden and pond more difficult and causing possible drainage problems and land slips toward neighboring properties.

The problem was how to contain the view within the garden. I decided to create two separate areas consisting of a water section and a dry garden. In front of the living room I made a large pond which I planted heavily with shrubs and trees to hide the encroaching vista of the neighboring houses and gardens. The existing patio was extended over the pond to create an illusion of increased space. A wisteria trellis was added to connect the house with the pond. Furthermore, on either side of my client's property there were major differences in the levels of the land. I therefore built a strong bamboo fence to the left and a concrete wall to the right. This wall was treated

❶ Above: View from garden
❷ Center: View from house
❸ Below: View from patio

with a grey textured paint which combined with the curving roof tiles to create a Japanese effect.

The position of the summer house offered a pleasing view of the pond with its *koi* and iris.

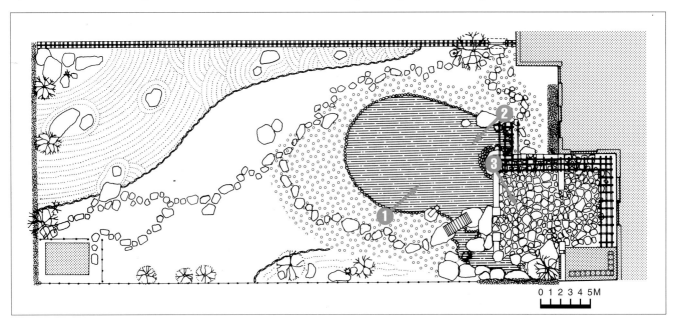

0 1 2 3 4 5M

Example 3

My clients were a retired couple who had recently moved to the leafy suburbs of Surrey, near London. They wanted their entire back garden transformed into a calm and restful Japanese garden. They asked me to create a dry garden, with a small patio area outside their living room. My design would place the patio at a vantage point from which to enjoy the various aspects of the garden, and bench seats and a barbecue on the patio would ensure full enjoyment of these. Although most of the ground was to be covered with granite chips, my clients asked me to include varied and interesting plant material to represent the seasons. The garden had to be easy to maintain, as they planned to spend half of each year abroad.

The garden shed was clearly visible from the seating area and the lounge, so to hide it I extended the exterior wall of the house. To make the wall itself more attractive, I built a large circular opening into the extension, behind which I planted a pine tree which could then be glimpsed through the opening. The garden was surrounded by a wooden fence, which I covered with lengths of split bamboo to create an oriental feeling. One third of the garden was devoted to plant material and the rest was filled with granite chips interspersed by stepping stones. I also included a very small water feature. My client, who had previously never shown any interest in gardening, suddenly became totally involved with his new Japanese garden. His wife could not believe it!

❶ Above: View from patio
❷ Below: View from house

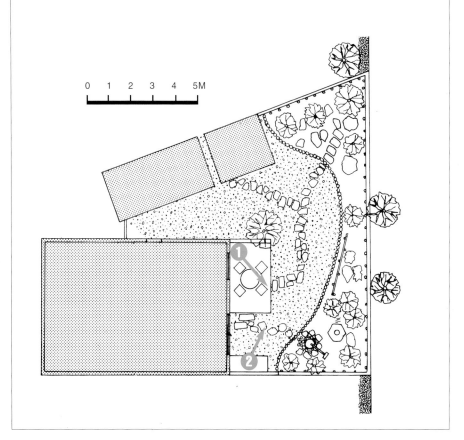

COURTYARD GARDENS

This style of garden is popular in Japan, since it can be made in almost any small and otherwise unusable area. The courtyard garden can create an illusion of space, transforming a corridor, a passageway, or a space between two houses into an interesting and unusual area. It is also useful for problem areas such as the exterior corner of a house where drainpipes or the side of a garage are visible. The design should be kept as simple as possible, with only one focal point. Overcrowding a garden with ornaments and plants should be avoided. Simplicity is definitely the best policy.

Example 1
The fortunate owner had a head start with the existing features of this city garden. The high walls surrounding the garden gave it great privacy and ensured that the proposed design would not disturb the neighbors. On two sides, the walls were beautifully disguised by a dense covering of ivy. This meant that only the wall at the rear of the garden needed a bamboo fence.

Furthermore, the existing garden had borders edged with lovely natural stone which I decided to utilize in the small paved area near the house. By turning the individual stones on their sides I was able to display them in a new and exciting way.

As the garden was very narrow I decided to emphasize its depth rather than its breadth. A meandering path of stepping stones was placed at the far end. To create an illusion of distance, suggesting an "endless path," the stepping stones were intersected at two points by simple bamboo fences, so that the path seemed to disappear behind the fence, then reappear beyond it at a greater distance. Lastly, a focal point was created by constructing a dramatic waterfall, which could be heard from the house, on the left of the garden.

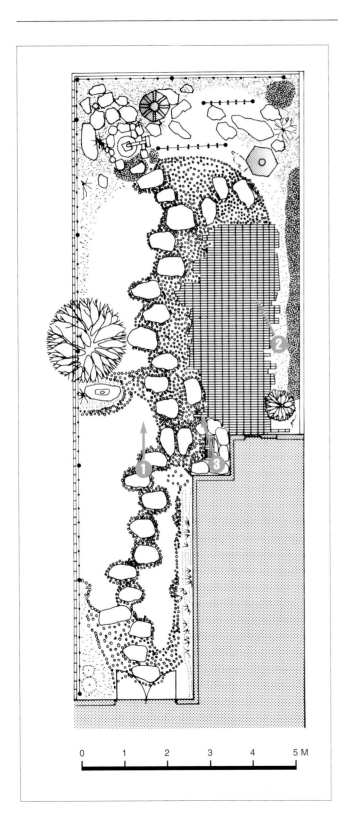

0 1 2 3 4 5 M

❶ Above: View from front
❷ Center: View from side
❸ Below: View from center corner

Example 2

Although situated near the picturesque banks of London's River Thames, the small garden of this townhouse was overshadowed by a neighbor's high brick wall which faced the owner's living area. The main problem was how to concentrate the viewer's attention within the garden and distract them from the high wall.

I decided to cover the lower portion of the offending wall completely, using an interesting bamboo fence with curved roof tiles. The existing brick walls to the left and right were disguised by split bamboo screens. An island with a stone lantern, plants and water basin provided the focal point.

As the owner had requested a simple viewing garden with very little maintenance, the entire surface of the garden was covered with white marble chips which make the garden look lighter and larger. Rectangular pieces of granite interspersed with *nachiguro* and lengths of bamboo suggest a pathway leading from the garden gate to the house.

❶ View from center

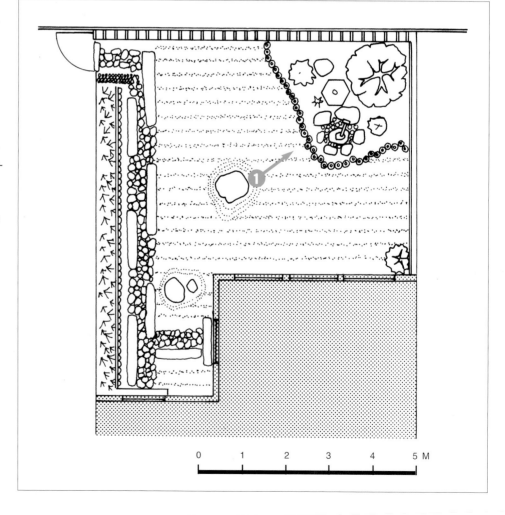

0   1   2   3   4   5 M

40

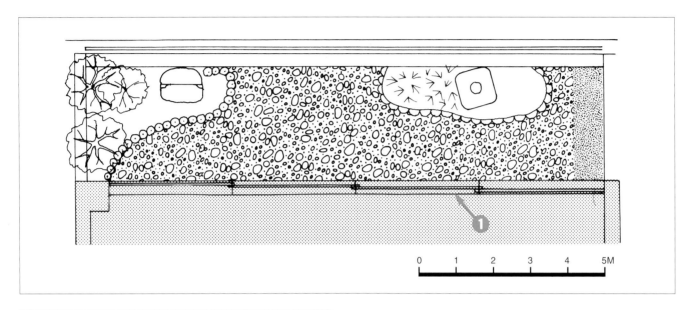

 is the plan diagram at the top. Below it is the scale bar.

0   1   2   3   4   5M

ROOF AND BALCONY GARDENS

As cities and towns become more crowded, and apartment buildings sprout up in areas where houses once stood, balcony and roof gardens are becoming increasingly popular.

Japanese gardens are the perfect choice for creating a sense of space on a small rooftop. Furthermore, there is no need to worry about a conflict with the environment, which usually consists of nothing more than a distant view and an expanse of sky. But this type of environment creates its own special problems. Roof gardens are usually exposed to strong winds that make it difficult to grow plants. In addition, roofs can only bear a certain amount of weight, which limits the amount of stone that can be used. Materials should therefore be as light as possible. If you decide to incorporate a water section into your design, great care must be taken to ensure there is no leakage into the apartment below.

Example 1

The owners of this very modern apartment asked me to design a garden to hide the unpleasant view from their bedroom window. The balcony, which was very small and narrow, presented a challenge.

With the addition of a wall made of white plastic pipes, the balcony became an extension of the living area. Large white sea pebbles made the area appear much lighter, while a traditional stone Buddha provided a contrast to the very modern stone lantern. The overall result is an atmosphere of tranquility.

❶ View from apartment

Example 2

This city roof garden is situated directly over a car showroom, and the owners were prohibited from removing the existing pebbles which covered the ground surface.

I decided to overcome this restriction by creating that atmosphere of stability which is usually associated with gardens at ground level. This is a very useful idea to use in the design of roof or balcony gardens. Bamboo fences contained the view within the garden area. Four plant containers were faced with slats of natural wood and two were placed at the far end to emphasize the feeling of depth.

At the entrance to the garden I placed a stone water basin over a square fiberglass container to hide the pump; this fiberglass container was also faced with natural wood. Stepping stones were interspersed amongst the pebbles to make the garden appear much longer.

❷ View from middle of path

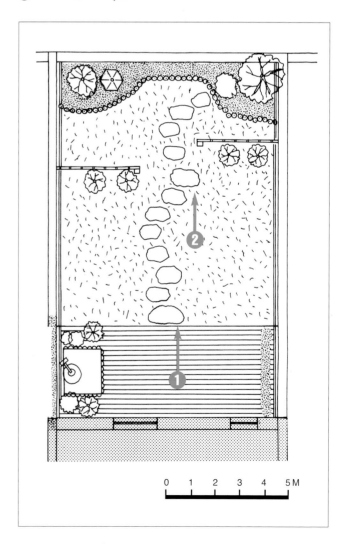

❶ View from apartment

0 1 2 3 4 5 M

Example 3

The owners of a triplex city apartment asked me to design a roof garden to be used mainly for entertaining. The stairwell leading up from the living accommodation to the garden divides the space into three distinct areas which I decided to emphasize in my design.

Each section has its own individual style. I retained the larger of the three areas as open space and covered the surface with artificial turf (sold by the roll) for easy maintenance and to solve the problem of possible leakage. A bamboo fence was erected to hide the view of the neighbor's garden. The existing plant containers were retained and extended with natural wood to create ample seating space for guests. Bamboo was planted in the containers to form a screen from the strong winds.

Oriental-style lamps were custom-made and interspersed amongst the bamboo to create an interesting atmosphere for evening entertaining. The weight of the materials used was evenly distributed over the entire space to protect against

❶ Above: View from right
❷ Below: View from center

excess weight bearing down on the apartment below. I paved the area on the other side of the stairwell and included a small water section with a stone basin. This led to a narrow corridor which was disguised by stepping stones set into marble chippings.

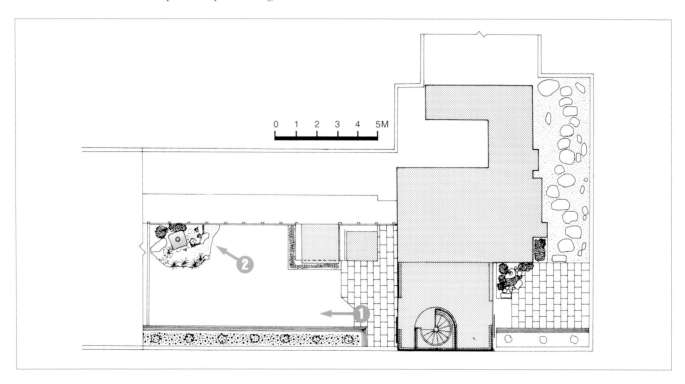

0 1 2 3 4 5M

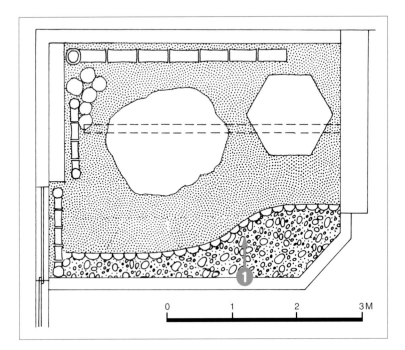

❶ View from front

INTERIOR GARDENS

Many people who live in apartments or town houses have neither a roof nor a balcony on which to create a Japanese garden. But this is not a problem. As long as there is a suitable interior space, such as the entrance hall or the area underneath the stairs, it is possible to create a strong Japanese influence without too much time and trouble. The main consideration is the avail-

ability of natural light. In the absence of natural light, you should avoid using natural plant material and create a dry garden using rocks, stones and garden ornaments.

I confront the same problem when I am asked to make Japanese gardens for conferences, exhibitions and private functions. They are relatively easy to design and execute and can create a very strong and distinctive atmosphere. Their temporary nature affects both the design and the materials used; some temporary gardens may only exist for a day or two. Since the display will not be permanent it has to be freestanding and must not be allowed to damage floors. By using artificial stone and fiberglass garden ornaments, both damage to these decorative elements and transport as well as labor costs, can be kept to a minimum.

Depending on the duration of the exhibition, you can use fresh or artificial plants, trees and shrubs. I sometimes incorporate fresh or artificial flowers into the design, as well, to add a touch of color and brightness. Live plants need to be changed on a regular basis, especially in an interior garden. The artificial light and dry conditions mean that plants without roots will have to be changed every few days.

Example 1
This dry garden is situated in a corner of the living-room of a city townhouse. A *shōji* screen has been suspended from the ceiling to create an impression of increased depth, so that it appears as if the garden extends beyond the screen. A simple bamboo screen fence with a small stone lantern, rocks and artificial plants work together to lend a most pleasing Japanese touch to the room.

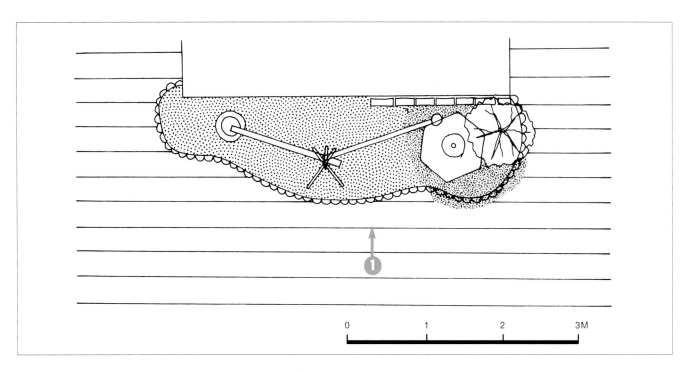

Example 2
This is the corner of a large entrance hall. The water circulates through a bamboo pipe into a stone basin, and the soothing sound of the water can be heard throughout the ground floor. A bamboo sleeve fence frames a stone lantern and some plants. Lengths of natural wood were used to make the border and the whole area was then filled with white pebbles.

❶ View from front

0   1   2   3M

Example 3

This garden was designed to be placed in the central hall of a large shopping precinct to celebrate Japanese Week. As the ceiling was high, I used very tall artificial bamboo. An unusual coiled rope feature complemented the modern architecture of the building. All the material used was artificial, including the stone, stone lantern and the stepping stones.

❶ View from left

❷ Aerial view

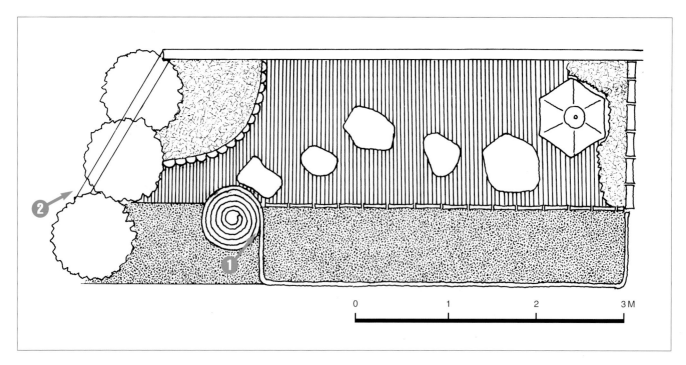

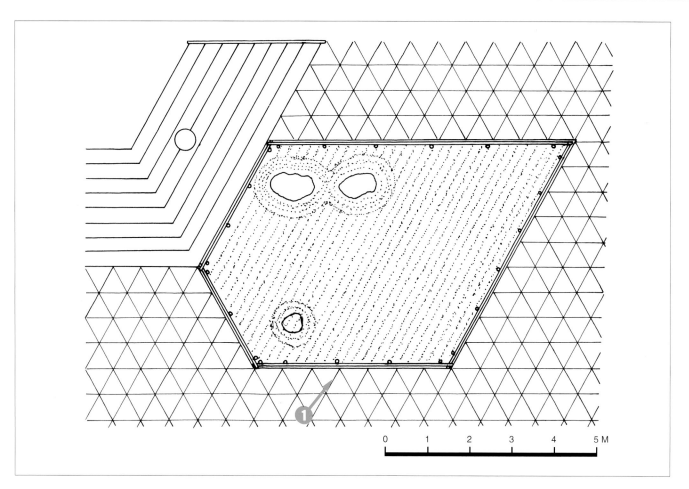

0   1   2   3   4   5 M

❶ Aerial view

Example 4

I was asked by the representative of a local government department to design a garden for the central area of a modern office building. As the building was also used at night, I included an extensive lighting system. The garden was required for two months and, as the central stair area was very dark, I decided to use only artificial plant material. Artificial stone was set into white granite chippings and the raked pattern was periodically changed. The design of the lighting system was also changed to create different effects.

❶ Above: View from right of living room
❷ Below: View from center of living room

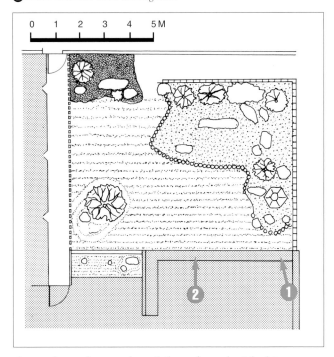

DRY GARDENS

The simple beauty and tranquillity of the dry garden can be striking in a Western home or garden, and has many advantages. It can be made in any environment and on a site of any size, so can be created in the stairwell of a private home as easily as in a large public park. The materials are easy to find and, since plants are not used, maintenance is reduced to a minimum. (The addition of living plant material does seem to work very well with Western-style houses, however.)

Nevertheless, a dry garden does have its challenges—one of which is that it can easily look contrived. Much thought and effort must go into the placement of every element, down to the last stone. The layout should be as simple as possible and the garden should be in balance with its surroundings. A dry garden is so distinctive that it is important to check that the surrounding area will be conducive to such a garden. Will its style conflict with its surroundings, for example, or will it be at risk from playing children or leaves falling from nearby trees which may necessitate regular garden maintenance?

If a dry garden is to be part of a larger garden, it is important to consider what percentage of the total site it will occupy. Because of its strong character, it is also advisable to separate it from the rest of the garden with a fence or a wall.

Example 1

My clients had often visited Japan and longed to have a Japanese garden. When they found this modern house in a quiet London suburb, they immediately realized that it was the ideal situation for one and so decided to replace the heavily planted front garden with its fish pond and brick feature.

The large windows of the living room overlooked the front garden which was at a slightly higher level, and the living room wall extended through to the garden. I therefore decided to design the garden as an extension of the living area. It was to be a dry, viewing garden since the back garden was used for entertaining and as a play area for the children.

Three separate planting areas were designed for easy maintenance. These represented rocky islands in the sea. By changing the raked pattern of the pebbles, the image could be changed from calm, gentle waves to a rough and stormy seashore.

48

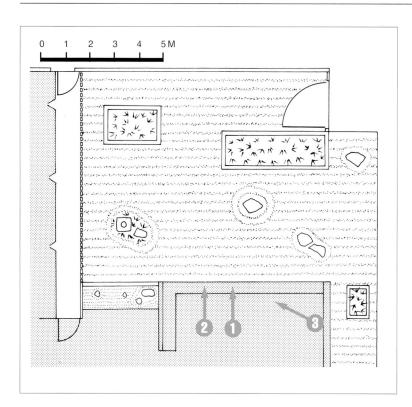

Eight years later the owners decided to create a simpler type of garden. As there was an extra plot of land to the right, the wall was extended to create an L-shape. To create the illusion of a tiled temple wall, the bricks were painted white with black vertical lines to represent wood panels. Curved tiles were placed on top of the wall. The three islands containing bamboo and azalea were retained, and five groups of stone were added. To connect the garden to the house I used a border of black *nachiguro* stones over which water gently flowed into a trough. An extensive lighting system was added for evening viewing.

❶ Above: View from house during winter
❷ Center: View from center of living room
❸ Below: View from right of living room

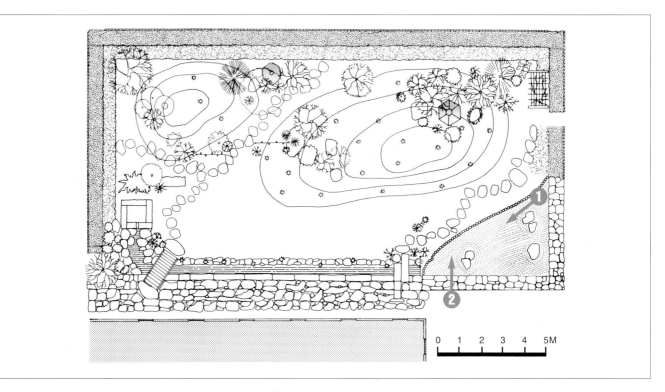

Example 2

A traditional old house, set on ten acres of the English countryside, was the location for this dry garden. As the existing garden had a very powerful, masculine atmosphere, I wanted to create a contrasting effect.

The area that I chose for the dry garden included a beautiful old weathered wall, built from local stone, which I decided to emphasize as a special feature. This was reflected by five very large pieces of weathered stone set into three groups representing three islands. Although the dry garden is very small compared to the total garden area, it has a strong presence and a powerful effect.

❶ View from dry garden

❷ View from house

❶ Above: View from stream
❷ Below: View from bridge

WATER GARDENS

Used in waterfalls, ponds, streams, water basins, and deer scarers, water not only creates movement and rhythm in the garden, but the sound of flowing water has a calming effect on the senses. It can be used to create either a distinctly masculine or feminine mood. But, as I have previously stressed, special knowledge is required to construct a water garden, and costs can be high. It is therefore advisable to engage a professional when embarking on the creation of this type of garden.

Example 1

When I first visited this garden it consisted of a flat grass lawn bordered by mundane flower beds. My client had visited Japan and asked me to design a traditional garden with a strong water influence in which to keep *koi*.

His other request was that he be able to hear the sound of water from each room of the house. For this reason the main feature of this garden was a very large waterfall which cascaded into a meandering stream.

Unusual rocks were used in the waterfall and set into the banks of the stream. A summer house was placed where it could offer the best view of the garden; it was made by a local craftsman, who also made the traditional wooden bridge.

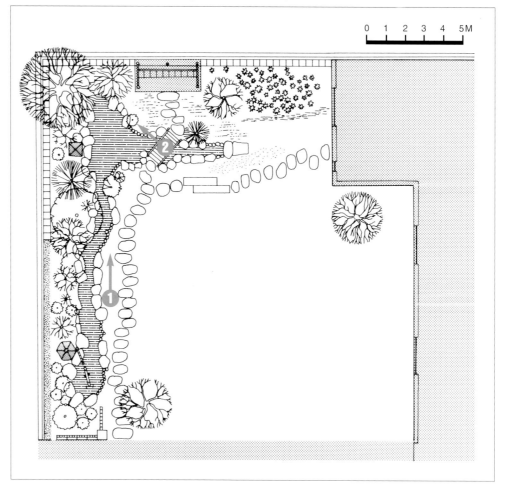

0 1 2 3 4 5M

Example 2

I was asked by a city council to design a peace garden in memory of the victims of the atomic bombs dropped on Japan at the end of World War II. It was to be part of a large public park. As water was to be the main element, I designed a waterfall to feed into a curving stream which flowed into the lake at the far end of the garden. In the center of the lake we built a small island on which were placed a symbolic stone lantern and a carefully trimmed pine.The shape of the lake represents the Chinese character for "heart" (*kokoro*). This garden has a very peaceful and calming atmosphere.

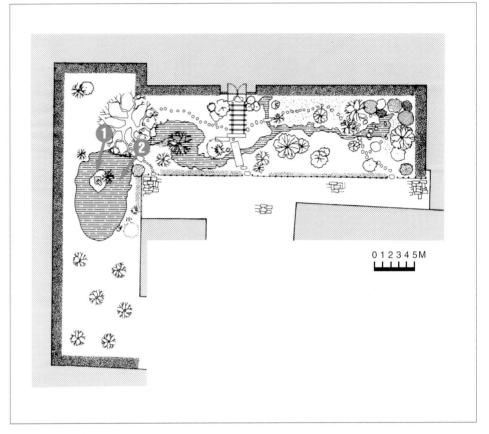

0 1 2 3 4 5M

❶View from back, left side

❷View from center, left side

❶ View from right

❷ View from front, right side

Example 3

The central courtyard of a modern office building was the setting for this garden. The area was enclosed by glass windows and was used for recreation by the office staff. In this kind of situation a traditional style garden would have been out of place, so I based my design upon the Japanese idea of simplicity. Water from a round concrete well bubbled through a hollow bridge into a large rectangular pond. The edge of the pond was designed to provide ample seating for the staff to watch the *koi* and enjoy the different aspects of the garden.

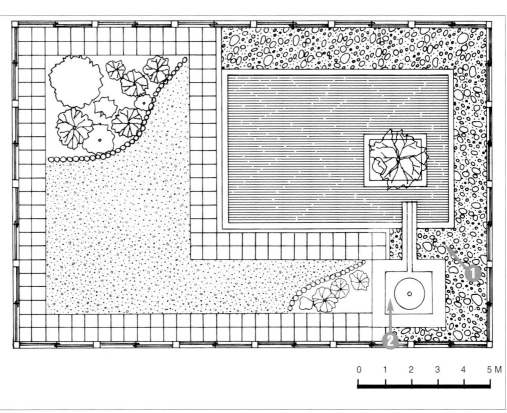

0 1 2 3 4 5 M

3 | GETTING STARTED

There are a number of factors to be taken into account when planning a Japanese garden, and a number of additional considerations that are unique to creating a Japanese garden outside Japan.

To create any type of garden, patience is a very important ingredient, but even more so for the Japanese garden. It will be three to five years before your plants mature, and three to seven years before you start to see the results of tree trimming, or moss growing on the rocks. There is always a great temptation to overplant, but you must allow the empty spaces to fill gradually. You will also need additional patience and restraint while performing maintenance if your garden is to develop as you imagine. Before starting, you must make a long term commitment. Keep your future plans constantly in your mind and work slowly towards the goal. In this way your garden will progress steadily and you will make fewer mistakes along the way. Also, try to plan your garden according to the seasons, otherwise you may find that by the time you have set your stone and water section, you have missed the planting season and you will have to wait many months before you can complete the garden.

DESIGNING THE GARDEN

Designing the Garden Yourself

For many people the usual way of creating a garden is to make it themselves. Even though this means that you can create exactly what you want, it is a far more involved task than one would imagine.

As previously mentioned, it will prove immensely helpful to the project if you have an overview of the various styles of Japanese gardens and are able to distinguish some of the main differences between them. If you have the opportunity to visit Japan and stroll through the magical gardens and museums of Kyoto, by all means do so. For most people, however, the simpler option will be to browse through books on Japanese gardens and culture. Even in the event that you decide to hire a garden designer, arming yourself with this knowledge puts you in a better position to judge his or her ability.

The next step is planning the garden. You don't have to be trained as an architect to produce a workable drawing, but you must make your own plan of what you hope the finished garden will

Although located in the middle of a London suburb, this garden emanates the sense of balance and serenity found in all Japanese gardens

Usually laid horizontally, here the Italian slate is vertical, making a wall of many facets—each a small resounding surface for the falling water

look like. The most dangerous approach is to try to make a garden spontaneously; it simply doesn't work. It is also a mistake simply to copy an old Japanese garden. Instead, absorb as much as possible from old gardens and use this knowledge to create your own plan. Don't be too ambitious about the scale and complexity. If this is your first endeavor, try to plan it in such a way that you can make it without professional help. (In Part Five there are plans of gardens that you can construct by yourself). You will need trees, shrubs, stone, and it is important that you choose these items yourself if the garden is to reflect your ideas and personality. You will also need perseverance. It is not only time-consuming to seek out the stone, but to place it in the right position and angle to achieve the desired effect will take many hours of work, but creating "something from nothing" ultimately proves very satisfying.

Employing a Garden Designer

Many people who do not have the confidence, courage or time to plan or make a garden themselves seek the help of professional landscape designers who claim to specialize in Japanese gardens. Recent years have seen a worldwide boom in Japanese gardens.

Many companies advertise that they specialize in these services, but be very careful. Besides seeking the best quality work for the cheapest price, you must also look for someone who is experienced, hardworking and trustworthy. Meet the designer and ask to see some examples of previous commissions before making a decision. Above all, you must try to find a craftsperson who understands and appreciates Japanese art and culture. It is therefore advisable to hire someone who has studied in, or at least visited, Japan.

When you have made your choice, you and the designer must spend some time and effort in getting to know each other. As the client, you must make clear exactly what your requirements and expectations are, and the professional must show

that he or she understands your wishes completely. There must always be this two-way dialog, and any misgivings or disagreements should be expressed at this stage. Only then should the actual design stage be undertaken.

When the design is complete, both parties must discuss the salient details until everyone is happy with all of the decisions. Finally, when this has been achieved, the client must stand back and leave the way clear for the work to be carried out unhindered. As much as possible, all problems should be anticipated and dealt with at the planning stage. I have found that quite often after the work has commenced the client may suddenly change the original plans, or ask for extra jobs to be done. This always causes problems for everyone concerned. The workmen lose interest in the project when their work is changed, and costs escalate.

In some cases the design and construction are done by two separate companies, in which case there is often a problem with the accurate interpretation of your ideas. I have also found sometimes that although the quality of the work is technically of a very high standard, the workmen or supervisor has no knowledge or feeling for Japanese culture, and the client ends up with a garden containing Japanese artifacts, rather than a Japanese garden.

I strongly recommend establishing a rapport not only with the garden designer, but with the contractors as well. I mention this only so that you will be wary of this potential problem.

FACTORS AFFECTING DESIGN

Whether you decide to construct the garden your-self or hire a professional, once you have chosen the garden site you must take all of the relevant factors below into consideration before you begin the actual planning and design.

Family
Unless you live alone, one of the most complicated and difficult problems is how to reconcile the needs of each member of the family. Children's needs, especially, should be taken into account.

Have a family conference, and let all members of the family air their views on what type of garden they envisage and how they want to use it. Is it to be a viewing garden, just enjoyed from inside the house or is it to be for entertaining friends at a barbecue? Do you have young children who need a play area or are you a person who likes to spend weekends pottering in the garden? The biggest challenge for the garden designer, whether ama-teur or professional, is to make everyone happy. But compromise is the key word and at some stage you must draw the line and proceed in the best way possible to satisfy the overall needs of the family.

During your family discussions, don't forget to consider the limitations of budget and time. How much time and money can you afford to spend at the outset and on annual maintenance? Also dis-cuss the actual work plan and timing. You don't want to find that your annual garden party coin-cides with the arrival of the garden contractors!

House
When planning your Japanese garden, you cannot ignore the relationship between the house and the garden. Your Japanese garden should be an exten-sion of your house. In Japan, gardens were designed to complement Japanese-style homes. Since very few of us intend to build a Japanese

Above: A bamboo fence is not only decorative, but hides unwanted views from the garden
Below: This tiny dry garden seems to be an extension of the house

house, it is crucial to adapt the traditional garden to fit your own environment or it may look incon-gruous.

If you have plans to build your own home, I would strongly suggest that from the outset you discuss the layout of the entire land, the house and garden combined, with the architect and land-scape architect. When an architect is asked to design a house, often the garden is only an after-thought, which makes it almost impossible to create a good balance and sense of continuity.

You may have been living in your house for some time before deciding to convert either part or all of your garden into a Japanese garden. This situation is more difficult than if you had planned a Japanese garden from the moment you decided to buy the house, as you will have already created a particular kind of atmosphere and the new Japanese garden will have a completely different feeling, which must be made to blend with the existing surroundings.

Another point to be remembered is that Japanese gardens were meant to be viewed from the interior of the home. Please go into the rooms from where the garden can be seen, check the intended view and keep the angle in your mind. The connection between the outer corner of the house and the garden is particularly important, and I would suggest erecting a bamboo fence, sleeve fence or plant cover to soften and hide this connection.

If you live in a city and are surrounded by high modern buildings, you should build some kind of wall to act as a divide or buffer between the two conflicting views, but try to imagine what your proposed wall will look like from your neighbor's side.

Visible neighboring properties must be considered when planning your garden

Neighborhood

You may decide to create your garden in an area where you are surrounded and overlooked by neighbors' gardens. It will therefore be desirable to build a wall. Before you begin you must consult your neighbors to get their cooperation. It may also be necessary to check with the local town planning department that your plans are within their regulations.

If you are making a garden in a suburban area where the gardens are in close proximity to each other, or where you are part of a larger communal garden, care must be taken that the Japanese garden does not disturb the general harmony.

Here, rustic fence is used to contain the view within the small garden

Japanese gardens are unusual and have a very strong atmosphere and can therefore easily become the focal point and clash with the surroundings.

If you are lucky enough to overlook a lake, river, mountain, forest or the sea, you may be able to incorporate this view into your garden using the principle of *shakkei*, or borrowed scenery. Yet even if you face a pleasant view, it would be prudent to check with your local town planning department or similar authority about any future plans to clear the area or erect a large high-rise building.

Often a wall is necessary to hide a view which cannot be assimilated easily into a Japanese garden, although sometimes it may be impractical to build a wall high enough to block such a view. The answer, in this case, is to build a wall which not only has an Oriental feeling but is also eye-catching: a bamboo fence or a natural plant hedge, for example. The strong character of the wall will stop the viewer's eye from straying and draw the attention back into the Japanese garden.

You should think of a wall not just as a screen but as an attractive feature in itself. Make your wall more appealing than the object to be hidden: for example, use Oriental tiles for a roof effect. The time spent on such details is well worth the effort. But remember, from the design point of view, the new fence or wall should not be the focal point in the garden, but should become the background or frame. And, as I have stressed before, don't forget that when you build your wall it also becomes your neighbor's wall. Before reaching the building stage walk around and imagine what view the fence will offer your neighbor. You may have to change your original design or use different materials to create a wall with which you will both be happy. The building of a wall or fence is a costly proposition—more costly than you might imagine—so budget carefully.

Above: The wall and roof tiles are a charming complement to this garden
Center: This garden employs the *shakkei* method of including the surrounding scenery
Below: The interesting design of this fence keeps the view within the garden

Environment

Of paramount importance when you start planning your garden is the existing landscape. Is your land situated at the top of a hill or in a low-lying valley? Is your house on high ground overlooking the garden, or are you living in the countryside surrounded by woodland or open, rolling meadows? Do you have a city garden or a penthouse balcony?

If you decide upon a water feature but you live at the top of a hill, it will be difficult to pump the water up to your garden stream. In a penthouse you will have the worry of water leaking through to the apartment below. In such circumstances you should realize from the outset that water is not a good option. On the other hand, if you are surrounded by high hills and there is a stream nearby, bringing a natural water supply to your garden will be a more practical option, and the water feature can be your focal point.

If you have a large area at your disposal it would be far wiser to set aside just one part for your Japanese garden, rather than attempt to make a large garden representing different scenes. It is not easy to divide up a large area of land into smaller sections or "views." If you make a mistake in the overall layout, there will be no unity or connection between the different areas.

If you have a small area of land but are encircled by large natural features such as a forest or mountains, it would be wise to consider the "borrowed scenery" technique. In this case you incorporate the view outside your garden into your own. This can make your garden appear far larger, as it seems to merge into the overall scene. If, however, your view is not compatible with your small area you could make a dry garden with rocks and sand to create a contrasting atmosphere. By setting larger stones in the foreground and smaller ones towards the back, you can create an illusion of receding distance and hence make the garden look much larger.

Whatever the existing landscape, whether your piece of land is large or small, whether its situation is high or low, and whether it has a good surrounding view or bad, do not despair. Just maximize those features that make your garden unique. Consider whether there are particular features of the landscape which you may be able to utilize. For example, are you situated close to a natural water supply and have chosen to feature a stream, pond or waterfall in your garden? Piped water is unnatural and can be unreliable, as you must rely on an electric pump for the circulation and supply. It is far better, if you can, to be able to tap the resources of a natural river or stream. But you may have no choice. On the other hand you may be surrounded by a forest or tall trees, in which case it may be better to create a dry garden with sand and rocks to form a contrast with the lush vegetation. Your neighbor's tall trees may not detract from your garden but actually add to the beauty, while a high decorative wall will not only exclude an unwanted view, but serve as a frame to draw the viewer's eye inward to appreciate the garden more.

Climate / Soil

It is also vital to determine the nature of the climate and soil of your proposed garden to decide what natural plant materials you will be able to use. For example, there is no use in planting exotic and rare plants only to find that they cannot survive in your particular conditions. If you move to a home in a new area and have no knowledge of the soil and other conditions, don't start planning your garden until you have had time to do your research. You may find that those camellia shrubs you so carefully planned to use will not survive in your garden.

All living plants need suitable conditions in which to flourish. To plant them just because they are unusual, or are a gift, or because you have always associated them with Japanese gardens, is to plant for the wrong reasons. If possible, your best plan would be to visit your neighbors' gardens, or your local garden center, to see what flourishes in your conditions and seek the advice of professionals.

Maintenance

As I mentioned before, it will take at least five to seven years for your garden to mature and begin to look as you plan and imagine. From the beginning you must be aware that your garden will require maintenance both during this maturation period and after.

Maintenance is necessary in any type of garden but, contrary to their reputation of requiring little or none, Japanese gardens require even more attention in terms of time spent and financial considerations. Speaking from experience, I have designed and made beautiful Japanese gardens, only to return a few months later and find them in sad neglect, with many of the plants already dead. If neglected for too long, trees will begin to get overgrown, and if not checked in time the only remedy is to pull them out and start again.

I would suggest that if you plan to do the general upkeep yourself, engage a professional two to four times per year to check and carry out the specialized work, such as the trimming of the trees.

If you cannot find professional help in your area, then from the outset you must plan how much time you will have available to look after the garden, and how much knowledge you will need in regard to the specialized care which may be necessary. For example, the trimming and pruning of pine trees requires a high level of knowledge and is very time-consuming. One tree may require an entire day, once a year, to complete. Even though you may have studied the techniques in books and feel quite confident about trimming your tree, the environment and material differ dramatically from one geographical area to another, and the same techniques may not be successful. If you don't have either knowledge or time, plan to

The garden at Sanzen'in, Kyoto

use plants, trees and shrubs which require the minimum of care, or make a dry garden.

Budget

Planning the cost of your garden is even more difficult than planning the cost of your house. You can spend from a relatively small to a huge sum and the outlay may be never ending. One problem, as mentioned before, is that once the garden has been completed the maintenance costs can still be high. Also, many of the expenses cannot be anticipated ahead of time. For example, when you are digging a pond you may find that the soil is unexpectedly soft, or discover an obstruction such as a hidden water pipe which will greatly increase the cost of the foundations. On the other hand, someone may have kindly offered you some cheap stone, but the cost of transporting it to your site, and the labor charges involved in setting it may be exorbitant.

Design
Professional fee: 15%

Construction
Materials: 35%
Labor: 40%
Transport and delivery 10%

Maintenance
You should plan on spending an additional 10% of the total cost of your garden per year on professional maintenance for the first five years, after which it will be less.

If you would like to devote a little extra to any one area, it would be wisest spent on the best possible garden ornaments, as quite often these are the focal points of your garden.

Because there are so many variables, it is extremely difficult to accurately estimate the cost of your garden. The fundamentals to consider are material costs such as stone, plants, soil, wall or fence, and garden ornaments; there are also labor charges, transport and delivery costs, design fees, administration charges by the architect, and if the professional travels from a distance, accommodation may be necessary as well.

A word to the wise: cutting corners by attempting to plan and construct the garden from scratch without consulting professionals may prove to be a false economy. Many times the amateur gardener wastes so much time, money and energy that all enthusiasm is lost before the garden is finished. It is far better to try carefully to estimate your budget and utilize professional help when necessary.

A rough idea of how to divide up your budget is as follows:

4 | DESIGNING YOUR GARDEN

This chapter will lead you through the planning and design of your garden and the selecting of the materials to make it. There are designs for both the *chaniwa* and *karesansui* style of gardens. You may either copy and make them following the plan or adapt them to suit your own tastes and needs. I have selected a size of three meters by two meters for both, since it is an ideal size to make alone or with the help of a friend. The size can be varied but I strongly suggest a minimum size of two meters by one meter, as an area smaller than this will be impractical from a design sense.

The *chaniwa* plans contain the items most commonly associated with Japanese gardens: stone lanterns, bamboo fences, water basins, water pipes, stepping stones and plants. The dry garden, by contrast, consists merely of rocks and gravel. The art in the latter lies in the placement of the rocks.

PREPARATION

1. As mentioned earlier, it is very important from the beginning to create a connection between the Japanese garden and the surrounding environment. With this idea in mind, go into your garden with a notebook and pencil and stand in the center of the proposed site and look around you. Jot down the view that you can see all around, such as the garage wall, tall trees in the distance or your neighbor's greenhouse.

2. The next step is to calculate the direction from which the garden will be viewed. Draw a rectangle in your notebook to represent a three meter by two meter site and draw arrows in the directions from which your garden will be viewed. If your garden will be seen from the house, go into those rooms and calculate the area that will be viewed and mark this on your diagram. Views are very important factors which will affect your choice of design.

PLANNING

In this section you will draw different designs for your Japanese garden onto graph paper and play around with them until you are satisfied with the final result. You will need a pencil, ruler and graph paper. The graph paper should be as large as possible, minimum size 30 x 20 cm so that one square will represent 10cm (scale of 1:10). This will be an easy scale for your calculations as 30 squares x 20 squares on your graph paper will represent your 3 meters x 2 meters garden.

Don't make just one design or try to make alterations on one plan. Use all of your ten rectangles, even if you are satisfied with a particular idea. Play around with the various items, e.g., move the lantern or the water section. In this way you may discover an entirely new and exciting concept.

When you have finally decided upon one design, leave it for a couple of days and then return to it. If you are still happy with your choice, discard the other designs and proceed.

Typical *chaniwa* style garden comprising all basic elements of stone lantern, bamboo fence, water basin, water pipe, stepping stones and plants

Left: When planning a garden, consider the surrounding scenery

CHANIWA (TEA) STYLE GARDEN

As the requirements and the environment of each reader vary drastically, below are eight different layouts from which you can choose different items and sections to create your own individual design. Or you may simply use one of the completed plans, taking into account the conditions of your site. For example, if the left side of your Japanese garden will border your neighbor's wall, you should choose a design to be viewed from the front and right side only—in this case, plan A. If your garden will be seen all around, choose plan G.

SYMBOLS AND PLACEMENT TIPS FOR ELEMENTS

Following are the symbols that you can use in your drawings for the actual garden elements.

1. **Stone lantern**
50 x 50cm (5 x 5 squares) Since a lantern is usually the focal point in the Japanese garden, I would strongly suggest that you obtain one if at all possible. The lantern should stand behind and slightly to the left of the water basin. Traditionally, one stone is placed in front of a *kasuga* lantern. If you are also featuring a water section it is most customary and effective to place the lantern close to this.

2. **Bamboo fence**
10 x 200cm (1 x 20 squares)

This is a useful device to hide a view or an object that you do not want to include in your garden scene, such as a garage or compost area.

Traditionally the bamboo fence is placed near the stone lantern. In a small garden it can be used as an ornament that separates part of the garden yet allows glimpses of the separated area, thus fooling the eye and making the garden appear larger.

3. Water basin
40 x 40cm (4 x 4 squares)
A water basin is another major focal point in a garden. It can be placed alone or in combination with the bamboo water pipe. If there is no circulating water supply, the basin should

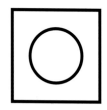

be filled by hand. Three stones are placed at the base to create a feeling that the basin is an integral part of the overall scene. (Exact placement of the stones is detailed in Part Five.) Shrubs are planted around the base to suggest a mountain brook or stream.

4. Stepping stones
30 x 40cm (3 x 4 squares)

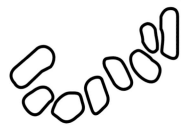

To achieve the asymmetrical balance characteristic of Japanese gardens, stepping stones should be set in an irregular pattern, to the left and right of a straight line. I have illustrated several different styles for arranging stepping stones (shown below) but, as long as you maintain this type of asymmetrical balance, you may prefer a pattern of your own design.

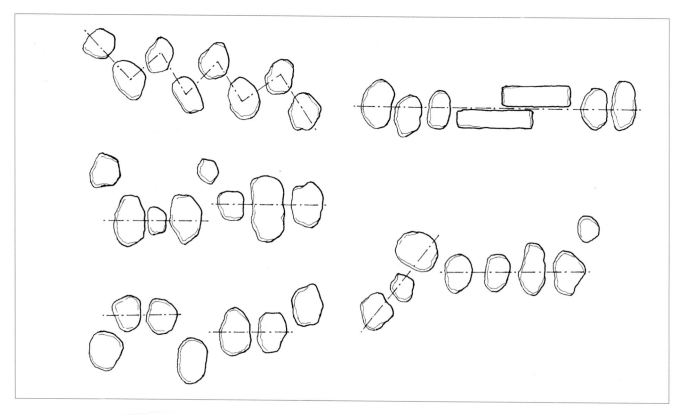

5. Water pipe

20 x 30 cm (2 x 3 squares)
A water pipe can be used in combination with the water basin or for purely ornamental purposes. When used without water, place stones around the base of the pipe to create the illusion that water is there but is hidden from view.

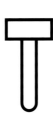

6. Plants

30 x 40 cm (3 x 4 squares)
Special care should be taken in the choice of plants, not only in terms of your design, but also for environmental reasons. Consider the site of the garden carefully, is it a problem area that gets relatively little sunlight, or does it suffer from a surfeit of humidity or wind? Bear in mind, too, that if you plant fast-growing plants you will soon lose the balance between the plants, the ornaments and the house.

Plants are the most difficult item to recommend. Unlike the other ornamental features, they are living materials. Your choice will depend on your soil conditions and climate. Also, it will depend on the amount of maintenance you feel prepared to put in.

Maintenance must be given serious consideration from the beginning. No matter how much hard work you may put into the design and making of your Japanese garden, if you ignore your plants and shrubs they will either die or pass the growing stage during which correct trimming can be done.

Most importantly, when designing a garden with plants, try to imagine what the plants will look like in five to seven years, and resist the temptation to overfill the garden now.

SAMPLE DESIGNS

1. First draw ten rectangles on your graph paper to represent the size of your garden. Either use my symbols or create your own to represent the items 1-6. Use the approximate sizes given for these symbols when drawing them onto your graph paper.

PLAN A

Items used = 1-6
Direction of view = front and right sides
Area to be hidden = back
Focal point = towards the rear of the left side

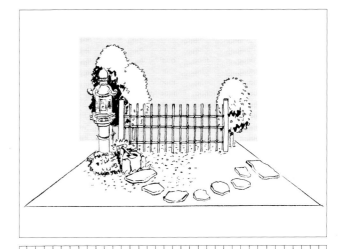

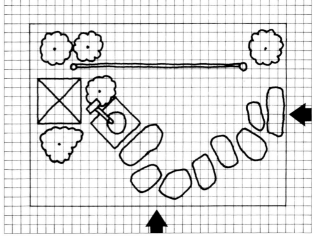

PLAN B

Items used = 1-6
Direction of view = front and left side
Area to be hidden = back
Focal point = towards the rear of the right side

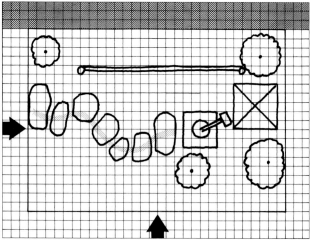

PLAN C

Items used = 1-6
Direction of view = front side
Area to be hidden = back side
Focal point = towards the front of the left side

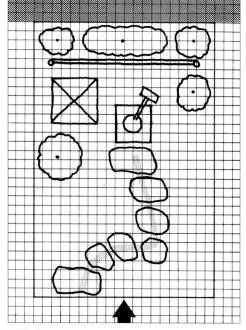

PLAN D

Items used = 1-6
Direction of view = center
Area to be hidden = left side
Focal point = towards the back of the right side

PLAN E

Items used = 1,2,4,6 (no water section)
Direction of view = front and right side
Area to be hidden = back
Focal point = stone lantern towards back of the left side. The stepping stones make the garden appear wider

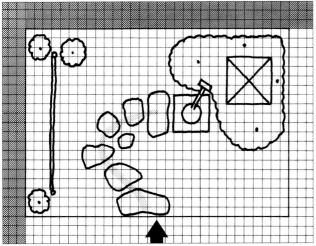

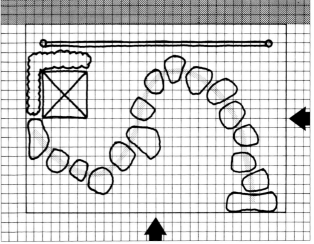

PLAN F

Items used = 2,3,4,5,6 (no stone lantern)
Direction of view = front and right side
Area to be hidden = corner between the back and
the left side
Focal point = water section towards the back of
the left side. An L-shaped bamboo fence encloses
the water section.

PLAN G

Items used = 1,6 (no water section)
Direction of view = all around
Area to be hidden = none
Focal point = stone lantern
This is a common design for a viewing garden
which can be look at from all directions, as in a
courtyard.

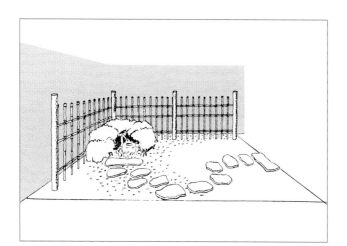

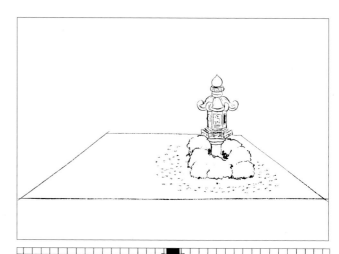

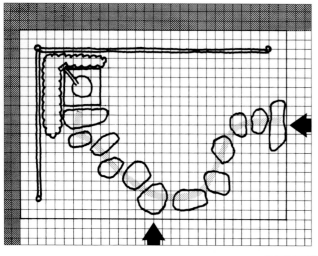

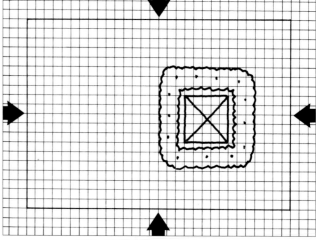

PLAN H

Items used = 2,3,4,5,6 (no stone lantern)
Direction of view = front, left and right sides
Area to be hidden = rear
Focal point = water section
The water section is situated towards the center of the garden and creates a strong contrast with the dry area. There is usually a high wall at the back. This is a very useful design.

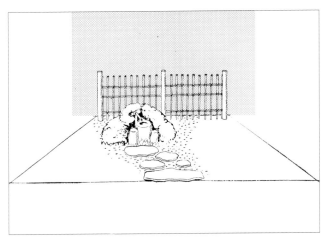

What the dry garden lacks in terms of elements, it compensates for in symbolism and mood. Space and balance are extremely important to the overall garden and with the groupings of stones. Much thought must go into the arrangement of each stone in order to achieve the proper effect of stylized naturalism.

Following is a guide to stone placement as well as two sample plans for designing a dry garden. In order to achieve an optimal design, I suggest you see page 72 for more information on stone arrangement from the *Sakuteiki* before you begin. For now, however, concentrate only on the layout of the stones. Information on dimensions of stone can be found in the Selecting Materials section on page 75, and tips for setting stone are given later in the Construction section, page 100.

SYMBOLS AND PLACEMENT ARRANGEMENTS FOR ROCKS

1. **Upright rocks**
Upright rocks should be buried beneath the soil to appear as if it has been in place for many years. Always use the same color and type of 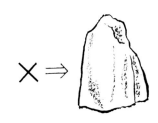 rock for both the upright and horizontal shapes.

2. Horizontal Rocks

As the name suggests, a horizontal rock should have a flat  shape and the top should lie horizontal to the ground. As more than half of its depth will be buried beneath the soil, the only important feature of the rock is that it has a flat top.

3. If you have two rocks, the most common combinations are:

Sometimes used :

Never used:

Three rocks

Four rocks should be placed in two groups of two.

For five rocks, the usual setting is either:
Two groups of two, and the fifth stone alone
    Total: five

or

One group of three and one group of two
    Total: five

For six rocks, the usual setting is:
Two groups of three

For seven rocks, the usual setting is:
One group of three, and two groups of two.

or

One group of five and one group of two
    Total: seven

Sample Designs for Dry Garden

Plan A

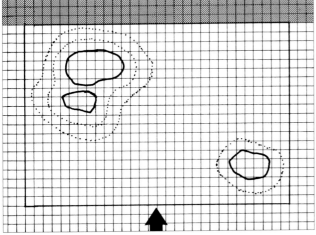

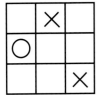

Plan B

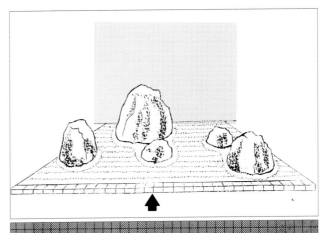

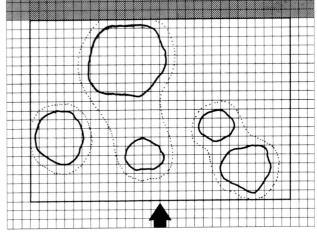

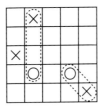

GENERAL DESIGN TIPS

1. The *Sakuteiki* recommends that you should always have a focal point to which the viewer's attention is immediately drawn. You may choose to base this on something you have seen in a book from an authentic old garden: a stone lantern in a tea garden, or a large arrangement of stones or a raised mound suggesting a mountain in a dry garden. To create the sense of unity which is so essential to your Japanese garden, the rest of your garden should be designed around this main focal point.

2. Do not overcrowd your garden.

3. Space and balance are extremely important in a Japanese garden. You may use the information on rock placement given in the preceding section to determine where to place plants and ornaments as well.

Making Your Garden Distinctively Japanese

ROCKS

The *Sakuteiki* offers both practical and philosophical advice on the placement of rocks. I would strongly suggest that you spend as much time as possible in deciding upon the grouping and placement of your rocks. They are one of the most important features in the Japanese garden and are a permanent fixture which, once set into place, cannot easily be moved, unlike shrubs or plants.

Once you have obtained your rocks, each one must be studied carefully from all directions and then placed into one of two categories: horizontal or upright.

According to the *Sakuteiki*, rocks should not be used alone but always placed in groups. However,

Moss-covered rocks along the shore of a lake

a group of three rocks may be placed so that two are close together and one is separate. The main upright rock must be placed into position first, and the accompanying horizontal rock must be placed in relation to the first to create a feeling of balance and harmony between the two. Together they must suggest one unified group.

Perhaps the most important advice is to avoid placing your rocks in a mechanical or purely scientific, measured way, as they will look as if they had simply been "dropped" into position. Try to achieve a harmony and sense of unity as if they were a group of friends interacting with one another. The *Sakuteiki* compares the desired effect to a group of puppies socializing and playfully quarreling with their parents. The subject rock is the parent and the supporting rocks are the puppies.

Position the rocks so that they look secure and established—as if they had been lying in their positions for centuries. One way of visualizing the finished effect is to think in terms of the human body, with the rock representing the human bone and the accompanying plants the connective tissue. Each is an integral and complimentary part of the other.

Traditional rules for rock placement are as follows:

1. If you are setting a group of two rocks, the hori-

zontal or supporting rock should be between 10-30 percent the size of the upright rock.

2. The supporting rock should assist the upright rock and help to create a feeling of depth and width.

3. The rocks should be buried beneath the soil to as great a depth as possible (approximately one-third to one-half) to look firmly established.

4. When deciding upon the positions of the rocks in relation to one another, always rely in the final analysis upon your personal judgement and not upon exact measurements.

The chain block, which has been in use since early times, offers a practical way of moving rock. It comprises a triangular frame of wood with a hook at its apex which is used to lift the rock.

Rocks of the same color and style are preferable

ORNAMENTS

Water basin

Three rocks should be placed around the water basin, and there are traditional rules governing their placement. These are:

1. One frontal rock should be set up at either end of the stepping stones leading to the basin or one placed in front of the basin itself if you are not using stepping stones. The rock should be hori-zontal and wide enough for two feet to comfortably stand upon. This is to create a solid base on which to stand while rinsing your hands. Set the rock so that it is approximately 1.5 to 3cm higher than the stepping stones. The water basin should be set at a distance of between 70-80cm from the frontal stone and 20-30cm higher.

2. The Candle Stone, upon which the candle rested (the candle was used as a torch), should be placed on the left side of the water basin. It should be about 15cm lower than the water basin.

3. The Hot Water Stone was used in winter to rest a bucket containing hot water for rinsing the hands in very cold weather. It should be placed on the right side of the basin. Rounder in shape than the candle stone, it should be about 3-5cm shorter and have a flat surface.

See illustration on page 94.

Stepping Stones

About 60 percent of the stepping stone path should lead in the intended direction while the remaining 40 percent offers a meandering route. Before securing the stones into their permanent positions, walk upon them and set them slightly to the left and the right. The gap between each stone should comfortably accomodate the width of one pace.

PLANTS

Before planting, please consider the following traditional methods carefully:

1. Do not place more than three trees in a straight row.

2. When looking at the garden from the main viewpoint, avoid having more than one plant directly behind another.

3. As seen from the main viewpoint, avoid planting material at equal distances from each other.

4. Do not place plants of the same size and height near or at equal distances from each other.

5. If you have three trees, plant them in one of the following combinations: either tall, short, medium or short, tall, medium.

6. If you have three different areas for planting, arrange them in one of the following two ways: either place the largest area to the front, the smallest area in the center and the medium sized area in the distance, or else place the smallest area in the front, the largest area in the center and the medium sized area in the distance.

7. If you want to plant a group of trees of the same variety together to create a focal point, they should be interspersed with smaller trees of a different variety, to avoid a symmetrical appearance.

8. When planting trees, never leave an equal distance between them. The usual ratio is 7:3 or 4:6. See diagram below.

9. When placing two plants, of either the same or different varieties, in front of each other, the one with the lesser density of foliage should be placed in the foreground to offer a "see-through" effect to the material behind.

10. If you wish to create an illusion of height or importance for an individual tree or shrub, either plant small shrubs close to its stem or trunk, or encircle it with a formation of rocks. The rocks will create a sense of solidity.

11. Always arrange your plants in groups of three, five, seven or nine. The triad is especially important, so if you have five plants you should place them as a group of either 3 + 1 + 1, or as a group of 3 + 2. If you have seven plants place them in groups of 3 + 3 + 1. Remember to alternate the heights and sizes of the individual plants within each group. Try to imagine a triangle with unequal sides and visualize the design from the front, side and bird's eye view.

12. It is important to emphasize the depth rather than the size of your garden. In order to create this effect, plant larger material towards the front and smaller towards the rear. The resulting effect of your garden receding distance will confuse the eye and create a greater sense of perspective.

13. When you want to feature a particular plant as a focal point, do not show it in its entirety but partially hide or disguise it by placing other material in front of the line of vision some distance away. This will create an air of mystery or surprise.

14. If you want to emphasize the shape of a particular plant, choose a variety which does not have strong and bright flowers or leaves which will detract from its shape.

SELECTING MATERIALS

Stone, ornaments and plants vary not only between countries, but within any one country. As a rule of thumb, keep the design, shape and color as simple as possible so that the elements blend into the overall effect of the garden, without any single feature overpowering the rest.

STONE

This is one of the most important and essential

elements in a Japanese garden. Finding suitable types and shapes to use is quite difficult. Ideally, one would go to the local mountains, ravines, or seashore and choose from the natural surroundings. But discovering to whom the land belongs, whether the stone can be purchased, combined with working out the logistics of transport from site to garden is an endless task. The best solution is to visit your local quarry, stone mason, or garden center and order the stone through them.

Some companies will let you purchase exactly what you see, but most will only let you decide on the type and rough size of the stone, as it is sold not by the piece but by the ton. To give you a rough idea, a medium-sized stone can be carried by an average-sized man, and there will be about 20-30 such stones in a ton. The price will usually include door-to-door delivery, but not the added cost of transporting the stone to the actual site in your garden, which may be some distance away from the point of delivery. The stone itself may be cheap, but the cost of transport and labor to move it from one part of the garden to another may be expensive. Stone is much heavier than it appears, and the larger the stone, the greater the time and labor that will be required.

Rocks

Rocks from mountain areas with rough angular surfaces are preferable to softer, smooth, curved

Rocks should have a natural appearance and not be cut into artificial shapes

rocks that have been molded by the motion of the sea. Rocks should never be cut level; the uppermost surface should be uneven so that, when placed on level ground, it creates an interesting effect. This also contributes to the illusion of depth. Note that between one-third and one-half of the entire rock will be set beneath soil level.

Rocks should be hard rather than soft and sandy, yet have a gentle feel to them; granite, for instance, has this feel, while marble is cold and unyielding. Gray and brown tones are the easiest to complement and blend in with the rest of the garden. Rocks should, if possible, possess the quality and appearance of age, i.e., they should have a mossy or weathered surface. The ideal size ranges upwards from a minimum diameter of 30cm. This 30cm size also represents a weight which is possible for one person to carry alone. Remember that transporting larger sized rocks will require either additional manpower or machinery such as a crane.

Rocks can be divided into two distinct groups: upright and horizontal. A number of wide horizontal rocks with a large proportion of the surface resting upon and beneath the ground is most desireable, as this will create a feeling of solidity and good balance in your garden. Avoid using too many tall upright rocks as they, in contrast, create a feeling of instability because only a small area rests upon solid ground. If you are setting only two rocks, the dimensions of the horizontal or supporting rock should be between 10-30 percent of those of the upright rock.

It is useful to note that many companies now produce artificial rocks in interesting shapes, both upright and horizontal. They are created from molds and often made of fiberglass, plastic or papier-mâché and, being hollow, are light and easy to move. They can look very realistic and are useful in difficult situations such as when very large stones are required. Artificial rocks are well suited for use in roof gardens where there is a problem of weight, and indoor gardens or sites where it is difficult for a machine to gain access. Do not mix rocks of many different textures and colors. Try as much as possible to use only one type, but avoid using rocks of exactly the same shape and size.

Wide horizontal rocks create a feeling of stability and good balance in a garden

Sand and Chips
The best quality is made from granite which is either ground into sand or into larger sized chips. If unobtainable, marble chips are a good alternative.

Stepping Stones
Stones that are to be used as stepping stones must be flat. If you are buying your stones sight unseen, I suggest that you order extra to ensure that you obtain enough suitably flat stones.

GARDEN ORNAMENTS

Ornaments vary greatly according to the material from which they are made, their age, and whether they are authentic or a copy. Your choice will depend upon your taste and budget. While antique Japanese artifacts are the best choice, they are expensive and difficult to obtain even in Japan. Today, however, countries such as Korea and China produce cheaper copies which are of a

lower quality than the real thing but can provide an adequate substitute. In recent years, some Western countries have also started producing quite acceptable copies. So if your budget is limited or importation is difficult, good substitutes can usually be found.

Lanterns
There are many different styles of stone lanterns, but the most common types found in Japanese gardens are the *kasuga* and the *yukimi*.

When choosing a lantern you should look for a pleasing artistic balance. When choosing a *kasuga* lantern, for example, this balance should be evident in the combination of the six sections: roof decoration, roof section, light section, support section, pedestal and base. The size and design of the lighting section will depend upon the area of the garden to be illuminated. If you wish to throw light onto a large area, choose a design where the lighting section is set high up.

The best material to choose for your stone lantern is gray granite, but lanterns are now made in a variety of different materials from natural stone to fiberglass or cement. Your choice will obviously depend on your taste and budget. As it can easily become a major focal point in your garden, I would suggest that you use only one lantern. If, however, you have a very large space available, two or even three lanterns can be used wisely to good effect.

A composition of a stone lantern, a water pipe, a water basin, rocks and shrubs in a *chaniwa* (tea) garden

A composition of a stone water basin, a water pipe and a bamboo scoop surrounded by stepping stones and a wooden path

Water Pipe

There are many different styles of water pipes available, but it is essential to choose one which has a natural, rustic quality. Instructions for making your own are given in Part Five.

Water Basin

There are numerous styles and materials available but your choice should depend upon the environment and the balance of the basin with the rest of the garden.

A round basin sits comfortably at the center of a square bamboo base

Pine and other trees at a garden center in Japan. The root, shaped into a ball, makes the tree easy to transplant

PLANT MATERIAL

The plant material available from garden centers and nurseries in Japan varies greatly from that found elsewhere. In photographs and books on Japanese gardens you will often see beautifully trimmed and shaped trees, sometimes several hundred years old. They have been carefully nurtured into unusual asymmetrical shapes from the time they were young saplings.

In Japan, garden centers sell large trees and shrubs which have already been trimmed and trained into shape and which come with a large root ball ready for transplanting. They are very convenient although very costly. Elsewhere it is almost impossible to purchase mature trees that have already been shaped. Even if you are fortunate enough to find a perfect specimen, your problems may not be over. Tree growth is affected by climatic differences and other factors so that even if you learned the correct trimming techniques, the results may not be the same.

The best solution is to buy trees that are four to five years old, and 150-200cm high. Try to imagine what you expect the trees to look like in five to seven years and, step by step, year by year, gradually try to achieve that effect. Remember at the beginning your tree will be small and will not have the correct balance with the garden ornaments nor the rest of the plants, but always try to keep the vision of the mature tree in your mind.

If you cannot find the type of tree or shrub that you have in mind in your area, you can purchase something that looks similar and then proceed to trim it in the Japanese style.

With regard to the recommendations for particular plants and shrubs, as climates and soil conditions vary so profoundly outside Japan, I have listed the most common varieties which are found in many different environments in Appendix 1. When choosing, you should consider the height, color, texture and seasonal changes of the plants. Most importantly, do not overlook the conditions of your garden; the plant must be able to survive in its climate and soil.

The two main plant materials used in Japanese gardens are pine and bamboo. Think about what kind of feeling you are trying to achieve in your garden when choosing the variety of pine. There are over six hundred varieties of bamboo worldwide, and if you visit your local nursery or garden center you will be able to choose the type best suited to your taste and garden design.

A grove of young bamboo

5 | MAKING YOUR GARDEN

BASIC TOOLS AND EQUIPMENT

Listed below are all the basic tools and equipment that you will need to make your Japanese garden in the *chaniwa* or *karesansui* style. Specialized items are listed under separate headings.

TOOLS

Wood for markers (4 sticks 30-60cm)
String
Measure, minimum 4 meters
Hacksaw
Saw
Wooden hammer (if possible)
Hammer
Electric drill
Hand drill
Garden scissors
Spade
Trowel   Spirit level
Bucket   Garden gloves
Broom   Rubber boots
Fork   Watering can
Rake   Weedkiller (if necessary)

MARKING OUT THE SITE
Materials:
4 wooden markers
String
Scissors

CHANIWA STYLE

Method
1. Remove all rubbish from the proposed garden site and weed if necessary. Hoe and turn the soil to a depth of 5-6cm and remove rocks and other debris. Level the ground. If weeds are a problem, treat with weedkiller. It may be necessary to remove those plants or shrubs in the immediate vicinity which may hinder easy access.

10 Steps to a *Chaniwa* Garden

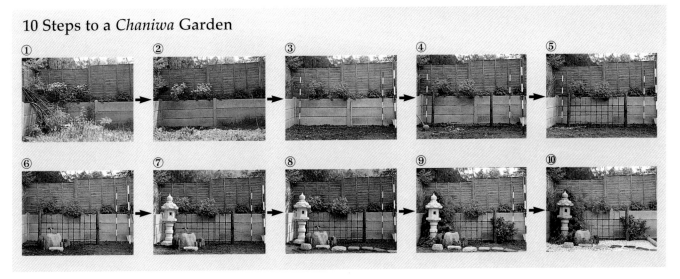

2. At this stage you should clear a small area close to the site for the temporary storage of garden items.

3. You are now ready to mark out your area. Hammer the four wood markers into the ground at a distance of 3 meters by 2 meters apart. Connect the four markers with string. This will represent the area of your garden. You are now ready to start work.

MAKING A BAMBOO FENCE

There are many different types and styles of fences used in Japanese gardens and they are made of either bamboo or timber. In this section, I shall describe the popular and easy-to-construct style of fence called *yotsume-gaki*. With a little experience and imagination you can create your own style according to your taste and needs. Bamboo is widely available; it is a versatile and pliant material, and is durable. The bamboo is usually tied with a special black string called *shuronawa*, which is made from the dyed fiber of the palm tree.

Above: A *yotsume-gaki* fence of green bamboo encircles a small dry garden
Below: Close-up of a *yotsume-gaki* knot

Materials:
2 rustic poles 140-160cm length, 8-10cm diameter
Wood preservative (if necessary)
10 bamboo poles 2m minimum length, 2-3cm diameter
50 m of *shuronawa*, thin rope or garden wire
20 nails 5-6cm
2 sticks 50cm in length (for markers)
Marker pen
Cement and sand (if necessary)

The rustic poles should be natural wood such as the trunks of young trees, and as straight as possible without blemishes. The cheapest and easiest woods to use are conifer and pine. Try to purchase poles with the bark already removed but if these are not available, remove the bark and treat with wood preservative.

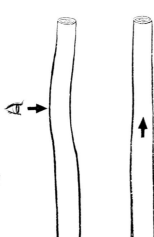

Ideally the bamboo should be straight and have a uniform diameter otherwise there will be a certain amount of wastage. Slightly curved lengths can be used, in which case turn the outward or convex curve towards the front view of the garden so that the angle of the curve is not seen from the front.

Method
To Place Markers:
1. Measure two points 50cm from either side of the rear left corner. Then measure 50cm in from these two points and, where they cross, hammer in your first marker. Repeat this process on the right side.

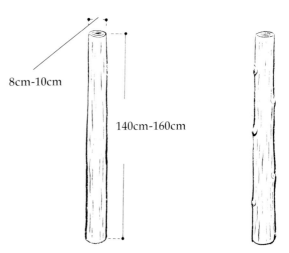

To Set Up Rustic Pole Foundation:
1. Find the top of the pole. This is usually the narrowest end but if the diameter of both ends are equal, check the direction of the shoot growth. Level this end with the hacksaw.

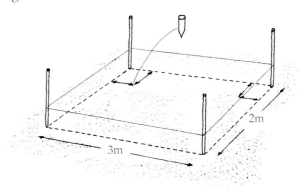

8cm-10cm

140cm-160cm

2. Measuring from the top of the pole, mark the 10cm point. Then mark the following points from each other: 25cm, 20cm, 30cm, 15cm. Please note that the 15cm mark will be the ground level. The amount that you leave below this level will depend on the type and softness of the soil.

3. Mark the center point at the top end of the pole.

4. Cut the bottom end of the pole to a point allowing sufficient length to be buried beneath the soil.

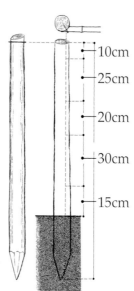

10cm
25cm
20cm
30cm
15cm

5. Remove the left side fence marker and dig a hole in its place the same diameter as your rustic pole. Allow sufficient depth to hammer your rustic pole into the ground to the 15cm mark.

6. When digging, pile all of the removed soil into one area to preserve the even level of the soil otherwise you will create uneven mounds.

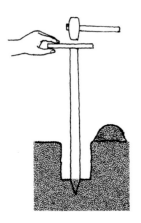

7. Put your rustic pole into the hole. Using a wooden hammer, drive the pole into the soil to the 15cm mark. If a wooden hammer is not available lay a block of thick wood as a cushion between the top of your rustic pole and the hammer. This will protect the wood.

8. Fill the hole with the soil pressing down firmly with a tool or stick to make a secure base.

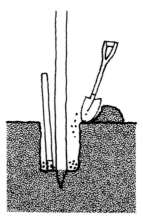

9. If the soil is soft, pour concrete into the hole to make the foundation solid.

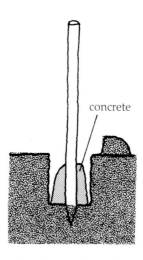

concrete

10. Repeat steps 1 - 10 on the right side of the garden site.

To Check the Level of the Rustic Pole Foundation:

It is now necessary to check that the rustic poles are in the correct position and at the right height. We do this by means of a length of bamboo placed horizontally between the two poles. This pole also acts as an additional support when making the fence.

1. Choose a piece of bamboo with an overall length slightly longer than the distance between the two poles. The bamboo should be as straight and as even as possible.

2. Lay this piece of bamboo to rest on top of the two rustic poles. Mark the points on your bamboo pole which lie directly over the center points of the rustic poles.

3. Drill a hole at either end of the bamboo at these center marks, drilling right through the pole. It is impossible to hammer a nail directly into the bamboo as it will split. You must always, therefore, drill the hole into the bamboo first with either a hand or an electric drill.

4. Put the nails into the holes and hammer very lightly through the bamboo into the top of the rustic pole so that the bamboo is only loosely attached.

5. Stand back and check visually that the bamboo pole looks parallel to the ground. Remember that this is only a temporary fixture to act as a support as you make the fence, and to check that the height of the poles is even.

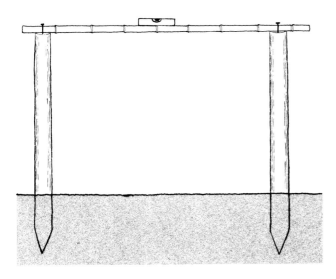

To Set Up the Horizontal Bamboo Bars:
First Bar

1. Select the straightest, thickest lengths of bamboo for the horizontal bars. The remainder can be used for the vertical bars.

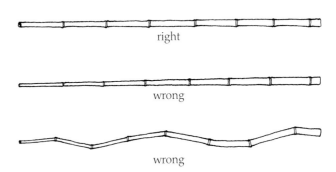

right

wrong

wrong

2. Make a diagonal cut on the end of the bamboo bar by placing the hacksaw just below the natural section of the bamboo and cutting at an angle of 30°. To get a clean edge, draw your hacksaw slowly over the bamboo as if you were cutting metal.

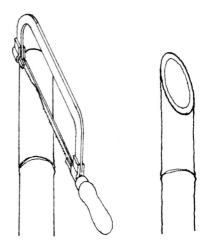

3. Drill a hole through the bamboo at the long pointed end of the cut.

83

4. Place this cut end at the back of rustic pole A at the 25cm mark and hammer lightly into place as before. This means that you will be working at the back of your fence.

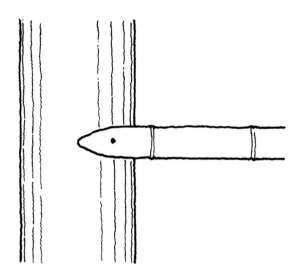

5. At this stage the other end of your bamboo pole should extend beyond the rustic pole.
With the hacksaw, make a diagonal cut so that the point of the diagonal will be roughly at the center point of the rustic pole. Drill a hole as above, insert the nail and hammer loosely into place at the 25cm mark.

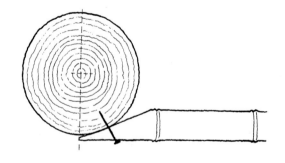

Second Bamboo Bar
1. Repeat steps 2 - 5 but start from rustic pole B.

Third Bamboo Bar
1. Repeat steps 2-5 but start from rustic pole A.

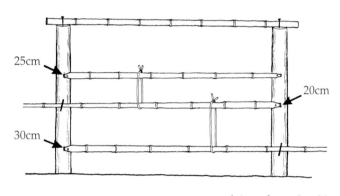

25cm

30cm

20cm

(view from back)

2. With the spirit level, check that the bars are approximately level. Remember that you don't have to be exact as you are using natural materials and absolute accuracy is not possible. Some adjustment may be necessary as bamboo varies in diameter and angle. You should make the final check visually.

To Set up the Vertical Bamboo Bars
1. Cut a minimum of 11 lengths of bamboo, each measuring between 90 and 100cm. You may even need more than 11 to allow for wastage.

2. Level one end by cutting as close as possible to the natural section break.

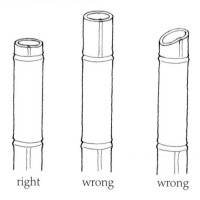

right   wrong   wrong

3. Tie a piece of string between rustic poles A and B at the 10cm mark, pulling the string as taut as possible. To ensure that the string is straight, check it with the spirit level.

4. Take the widest piece of bamboo and push it into the ground at the halfway mark between the two rustic poles. It should rest inside and against the horizontal bars. Hammer into place as before, until the top of the bamboo is level with the string. Remember to use a wooden hammer or block.

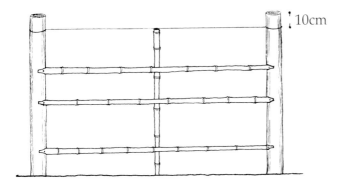

10cm

5. Now hammer a straight piece of bamboo inside and as close as possible to rustic pole A.

gap

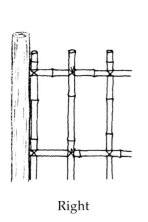 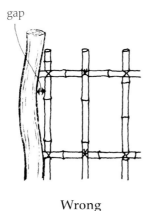

Right   Wrong

6. Repeat step 5 next to rustic pole B.

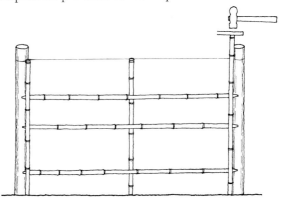

7. Place the eight remaining bamboo bars at equal distances between the three bars you have just hammered into position, i.e., four on either side of the center point. Place the first of these bars outside the fence, the second one inside, alternating each time.

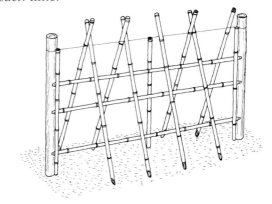

8. If the bamboo bars vary in diameter, place the thickest bamboo towards the center, and the others graduating outward from largest to smallest. This will create a pleasing sense of balance.

9. At this stage the bars are not fixed, but are simply resting in place. Stand back and visually check that the distances between them appear equal. Adjust if necessary.

10. Hammer the bars into place as before until they are all level with the string.

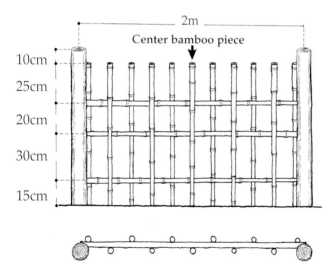

It must be stressed that these are natural materials. The sizes are never uniform and therefore my measurements are only approximate and are meant to be treated as such. Please check your fence visually and, as long as it appears to be level and has a pleasing sense of balance, that is sufficient.

To Tie the Knots on the Bamboo Fence
Preparation of the black string (*shuronawa*)
1. The string is sold in hanks. Find a length of wood to use as a reel, then unravel each hank and wind the string onto the reel.

2. Soak the string in a basin of cold water for about 30 minutes. This will not only make the string softer and easier to manipulate but, when it dries, it will shrink and make your knots tighter and more secure.

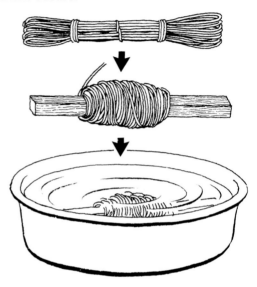

There are many different styles of knots used in the making of garden fences, but the one I have chosen is the easiest and most suitable for the *yotsume-gaki* style of fence. It is called *ura-jūmonji-aya*, or back-cross knot. The diagrams are easy to follow and after a few attempts you should be able to make the knots quickly and confidently.

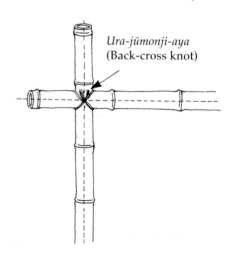

Ura-jūmonji-aya (Back-cross knot)

To Tie the Knot
1. Hold the end of the string in your right hand and pass it behind the bamboo intersection.

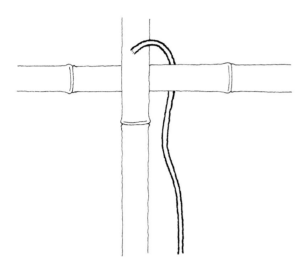

2. Grasp the string a few centimeters from the end with your left hand and pull it diagonally across the front and over to the left. Now bring it up, under and behind the intersection and push the end under the loop at the back.

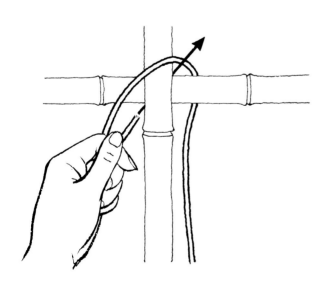

3. Let go of the string and grasp the end. Pull it in an upward, diagonal movement from the right side to the left. It is important to pull in an upward diagonal movement rather than a horizontal one if you are to be able to tighten the knot.

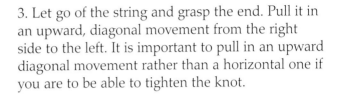

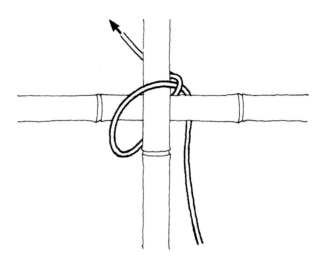

4. To tighten the knot, pull the left hand upwards and the right hand downwards. Check from behind that you have created a diagonal cross at the intersection.

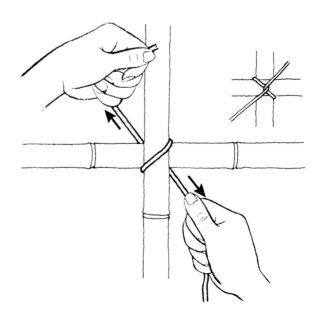

5. Bring your left hand, which is still holding the end of the string, diagonally downwards, across the front and towards the right side.

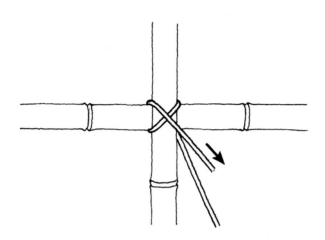

6. Pull the string taut. Let go of the end of the string while pressing your left thumb against the string at the center of the intersection. The end attached to the reel is still in your right hand. Now slip it under the short end and place in the left hand. Keep your thumb pressed on the intersection.

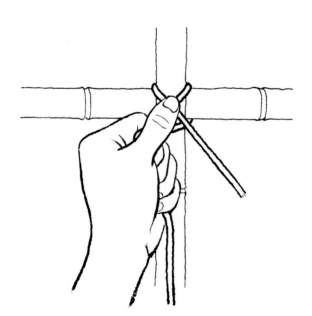

7. Now bring the reel end to make a loop around the short loose end in an over-and-under movement.

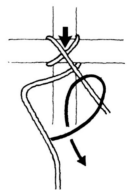

8. Push this loop upwards so that it rests against the top of the intersection. The short end will be resting on the top of the loop.

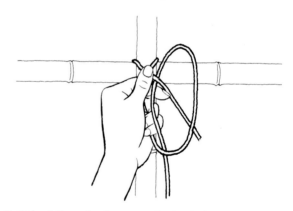

9. Still holding the loop with the left thumb, bring the right hand behind the left hand and pull the string in an upward, diagonal direction from right bottom to left top.

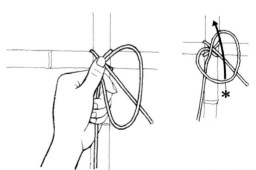

10. Still holding the end in the right hand, push it through the loop from the back to the front.

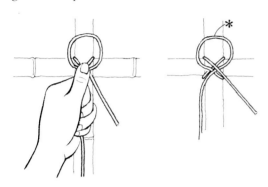

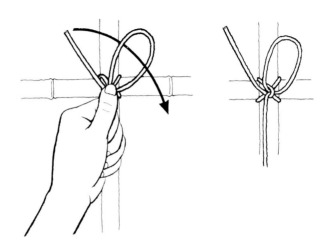

11. Grasp the end with the right hand and pull gently. It is important to have maintained the pressure with your left thumb continuously until this stage.

12. This pulling action will make the loop smaller. When it is the size of your thumb, grasp both ends of the string in your hand and pull simultaneously very gently, at the same time releasing the pressure applied by your left thumb.

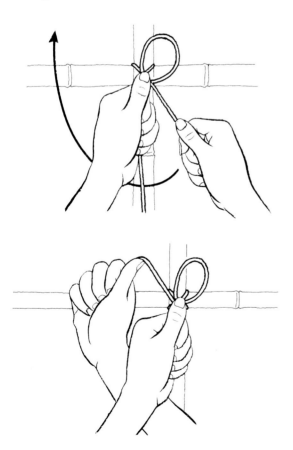

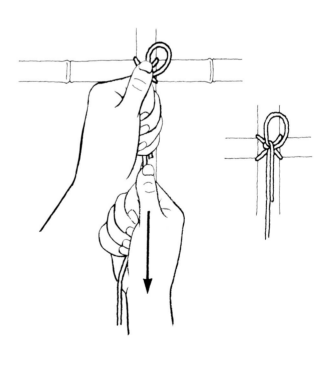

13. Cut both ends of the string 3cm from the knot.

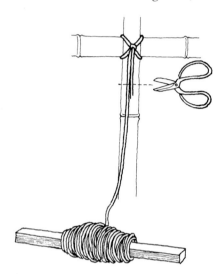

14. Continue at each bamboo intersection. You will have to work at the front and back of your fence as the knots are made onto the vertical bamboo bars. The finished effect will have the knots alternating towards the back and the front.

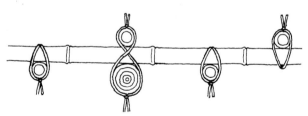

15. Now you can remove the top bamboo bar support. Your bamboo fence is now complete.

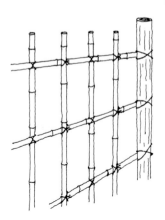

MAKING THE WATER PIPE

Traditionally, water pipes were made from bamboo as it was widely available and its stem is hollow and divided into sections. If a hole is made through the sections a natural water pipe is created. If you are not fortunate enough to have a natural water supply, you can create an effective system using an electric pump with a plastic pipe leading to the bamboo water pipe.

Materials

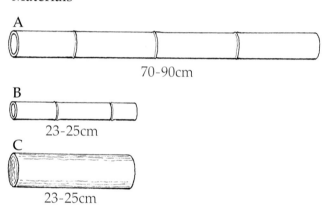

A

70-90cm

B

23-25cm

C

23-25cm

1 piece of bamboo 70-90cm length, 4-6cm diameter (bamboo A)
1 piece of bamboo 23-25cm length, 4cm diameter (bamboo piece B). It is essential that piece B has at least one or two naturally divided sections.
1 cylindrical piece of wood 23-25cm length, 7-10cm diameter. A rustic pole (length of natural wood, such as the trunk of a young tree) can be used.
Water pump
Plastic pipe (diameter to fit inside bamboo pipe)
Waterproof wood glue sealer
Water flow control tap
Chisel
Metal rod

Method

1. In bamboo A make a hole through all divided sections. To do this, place one end of a metal rod inside the bamboo, against the first section, and hammer the rod until it appears at the other end of the bamboo.

2. Make a diagonal cut on one end of piece A.

3. You will need to remove a small rectangular section from this diagonal end. Place the hacksaw 10cm from the shortest side of the diagonal and saw a length of 2-3cm.

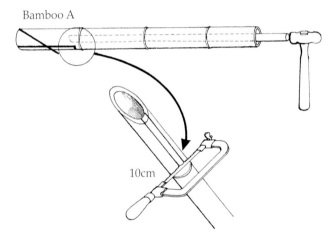

Bamboo A

10cm

4. Placing your chisel against each end of this cut, gently beat out the section with the hammer. It will leave a rectangular hole of 2-3cm x 10cm.

5. In bamboo B, break through the divided sections as above.

6. Cut the end on the diagonal as above but be sure that this cut does not pass through any natural bamboo sections, or these will stop the water from flowing smoothly through the pipe. Please note: there must be at least one natural section between the straight end of the pipe and the beginning of the diagonal cut on the other end.

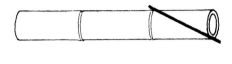

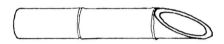

7. Make a hole halfway through the wooden cylinder at the central point with an electric drill. The diameter of the hole should be the same as that of bamboo A. Try and make the hole as tight a fit as possible.

8. Now make a second hole in the wooden cylinder at an 80° angle to the first hole. (This will mean that the second hole is not directly underneath the first.) The diameter of the hole should be the same as that of bamboo B. The two holes must intersect.

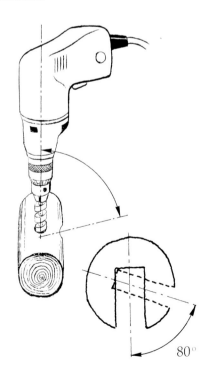

80°

9. Push the plastic pipe through the center of bamboo A from top to bottom. Then push it through the wooden cylinder and lastly through bamboo B.

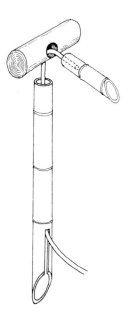

10. Pull the pipe and push both pieces of bamboo firmly into the holes in the wood cylinder. It is important that the pipe does not extend beyond the end of bamboo B but ends just past the natural wood section of the bamboo. The other end of the pipe will eventually be connected to the pump. The amount of spare pipe will depend on the height of the water basin and the distance from the pump.

11. Seal the bamboo/wood connections with the waterproof wood sealer.

12. Connect the flow control tap to the length of pipe between the water spout and the pump. The position will depend on the eventual distance between the two.

13. You cannot install the water spout until the water basin is in place. The end of the water spout (bamboo B) should lie approximately 5-10cm above the rim of the basin.

SETTING THE WATER BASIN

The water basin is the most popular way of including a water section in your garden and it is not essential to use it in combination with a water spout.

Materials
1 plastic or fiberglass container 30-50cm diameter, 30cm depth (The shape should suit the shape of the water basin)
1 stone basin
10 bricks
Rustic poles cut in uneven lengths between 20-30cm
3 pieces of stone, shaped as in illustrations A, C and D respectively.
Cement
Sand

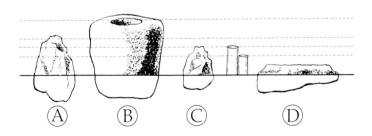

Ⓐ   Ⓑ   Ⓒ   Ⓓ

Method
1. Dig a hole in the soil the size of the plastic container and place the container into the hole making sure that the top edge is at soil level.

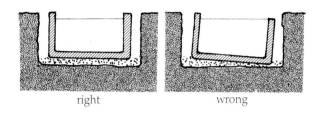

right   wrong

The bottom of the container should rest completely flat on the soil. To verify this fill the container with water and check to see if the water level is level with the soil.

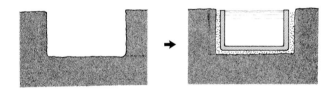

2. Fill the gaps between the container and the edges of the hole with soil and press down with a stick or similar tool to make a firm foundation.

3. Connect the plastic pipe from the water spout to the pump and place the pump into the plastic container.

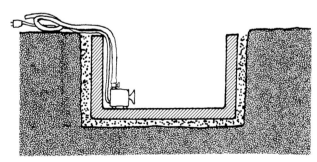

4. Build up the bricks inside the plastic container.

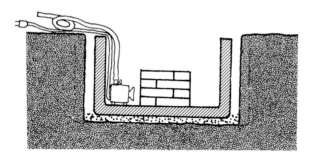

5. Place the water basin (B) on top of the bricks and check to see if it is level.

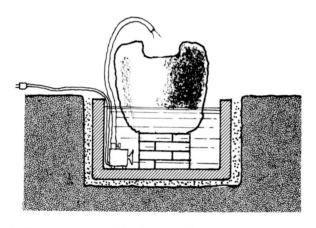

6. Place stones A, D, C around the water basin, B. For positions, see drawing below.

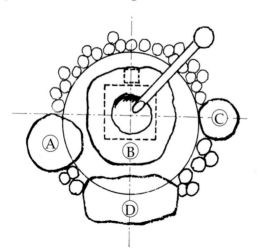

7. Place the rustic poles between the stones, remembering that they should be of unequal length to give a natural effect.

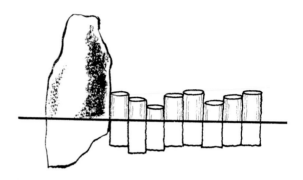

8. Hammer the water spout into position so that the end of the spout lies directly over the center of the water basin (B), 5-10cm above the top rim of the basin. If the ground is soft, fill the hole with cement. It is important to check that the hose is not twisted.

9. Fill the plastic container with water and switch on the electric pump. Control the flow of water from the water pipe into the basin by means of the control tap, so that it flows very gently. The water should not pour in a steady stream, but gently drip into the center of the water basin.

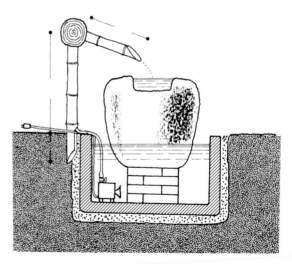

SETTING THE STONE LANTERN

There are numerous styles, shapes, materials and qualities to choose from, but the style I have suggested is the *kasuga tōrō*, the tall upright pedestal style, which is the most popular and authentic.

A *kasuga* lantern is the focal point of this "tea" garden

The basic *kasuga*-style stone lantern is divided into six separate sections, each one resting upon the other.

1.Decoration for roof

2.Roof section

3.Light section for candle

4.Support section

5.Pedestal

6.Base

Materials
Stone lantern
Cement
Sand
Spirit level
Stones approximately 6-8cm diameter. They may be bricks or cobblestone

Method
1. Dig a hole in the soil to a depth of 20cm and with a slightly larger diameter than the base of the stone lantern. Fill the hole with the stones and place the sand in the gaps between the stones so they will not move. This will make it easier to create a level base. Beat down firmly to make a solid foundation.

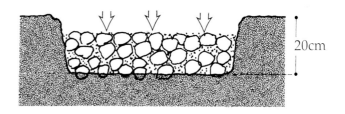

20cm

2. Place the base of the lantern on top of the foundation. Before proceeding any further, use a spirit level to check that it is completely level .

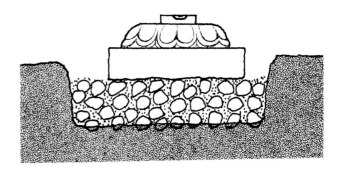

3. Place cement onto the top of the lantern base in the area where the second section of the lantern will rest.

4. Place the second section into position and repeat the process of checking the level carefully and adding cement until all six stages of your lantern are in position. It is important to check visually after each stage by standing at least 2 meters from the lantern and checking the angle from many different directions to ensure that it is centrally placed and not leaning. Please check also that each section is turned the right way up and all are in the correct order, since it is very easy to make a mistake.

SETTING THE STEPPING STONES

The idea to keep in mind when laying your stepping stones is that they should be easy to walk upon, so the distance between two stones should equal one step or pace. Do not place them in a straight line but think of the walking pattern and set them slightly to the left and right. Before securing them into their permanent positions, walk upon them and adjust if necessary.

Materials
10-15 stepping stones, 30-50cm in diameter. Choose a solid rather than sandy stone. One side of the stone should be flat (to walk upon) Small rocks or pebbles 6-8cm diameter to serve as a base for each stepping stone
Sand

Method
1. Following the diagram you drew in the design section, lay your stepping stones on the soil in the design you have chosen. Walk over them several times adjusting the distances and positions until the spaces between them feel comfortable. You should not have to take giant strides or tiny steps. At this stage the stones will move when you step on them.

2. When you are satisfied with the positions you can start to dig the holes. Each hole should be the same diameter as the stepping stone. The depth should be calculated in such a way that when the stones are in their final positions more than half of the height will be buried beneath the soil level. Remember to take the depth of the pebble base into consideration.

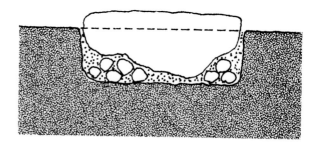

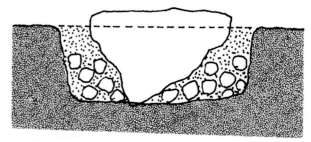

3. Place a layer of pebbles into each hole and hammer them into place to make a firm base.

4. Fill the spaces between the pebbles with a layer of sand.

5. Place the stepping stones into position and fill any gaps with sand.

6. Check the level of each stepping stone and correct if necessary. When you are satisfied, make sure that the area between the edge of the soil and the stepping stones is completely filled with sand so that they will not move at all when walked on. You can press the sand into position with a stick.

Planting

The materials that I recommend have a traditional Japanese feeling, and are readily available from good garden centers. They are also easy to grow and maintain. Should you have a problem obtaining your first choice, or find that you prefer a substitute, I have included a list of alternatives in Appendix 1.

Generally, planting is best carried out in early spring, before new buds appear, or in the fall, before the weather gets cold. For many trees, the latter is preferable, since it gives them a chance to establish themselves before new spring growth. It

is best to plant deciduous trees after they have shed their leaves.

To overcome the fact that the newly planted young trees and shrubs will not have a good sense of balance when compared to the stone, ornaments and other features in the garden, you may wish to plant some temporary material until your plants get larger.

Materials

1. Trees 1.5-2m - Japanese white pine (*Pinus parviflora Sieb et Zucc*) or Maple tree (*Acer Linn*) or Cherry tree (*Prunus serrulata*)
2. Shrubs 50cm-lm - *Fatsia japonica Decne* or Japanese Aucuba (*Aucuba japonica Thunb*) or *Mahonia japonica DC*
3 Small shrubs - *Spiraea cantoniensis Loun* or Rhododendron Kaenpferi or *Pieris japonica D. Don*

For items 2 and 3 you may wish to choose specimens of the same or different varieties.

Method

1. Once you have collected all the shrubs and trees, you should stand them in the correct positions in the garden to visualize the overall effect. Try to place them at the correct angle as well. Walk around and look at them from many different viewpoints. Now is the time to change your mind and alter the location rather than dig them up at a later stage and risk possible damage.

2. The general rule is that trees are planted behind the stone lantern, shrubs are planted between the different stones and smaller shrubs are planted in front of the stones or wood edging (made with the rustic poles). Placing the smaller shrubs at the front creates a softer effect and the object is not seen in its entirety.

A close-up of the basic elements of a "tea" garden

3. When you are satisfied with the positions of your plant material, use a stick as a marker and draw a circle in the soil for each plant. The size should be the approximate diameter of the root ball, so you will know how large to dig your hole.

4. Now move all the plants to a storage area for safety. (If plants are left close to the working area where you are digging, they usually get showered with soil and can be damaged.)

5. Dig each hole a little larger and deeper than your marked area and pile the soil which you have removed into a neat mound close to the hole.

6. Leave a small raised mound of soil at the bottom of each hole. The root of the plant will rest on this raised area. You may want to change the angle of the plant and if it is planted flat with the soil tightly packed around the root, it will be extremely difficult to move.

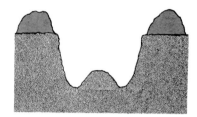

7. Add some peat moss and top soil to the mound of soil you have removed. The amount used will depend upon the condition of the soil. If, for example, it is poor in nutrients, you will need a high content of peat moss.

8. Lower the plant onto the raised mound in the hole, and when you are satisfied with its position and angle, add the mixed soil until it reaches about halfway up the root ball. Pack the earth firmly with a stick or similar tool to make a firm base, and then fill the rest of the hole to ground level. Pack the soil again and tread down firmly.

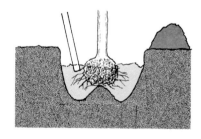

9. When the soil is level, make a small bank of soil about 10-15cm high that will encircle the plant completely. It should be about the same circumference as the filled hole.

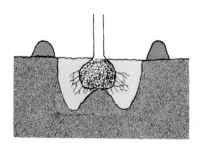

10. Water the plant until the water level reaches the top of the soil bank. Wait till the water disappears and repeat this process two or three times.

Completed garden

Normally about one or two months later, you will see signs of new root growth and indications that the plant is established. For example, there will be new bud growth, or the plant will look sturdier. You can then remove the bank of soil.

Method

Below are the materials you will need to make a dry garden. The rocks should all be of the same type and color; gray or earthen shades are best. Two should have a strong, sturdy, upright shape, while the remaining three should be flat. They should be between 50cm and 70cm in diameter, the maximum size for one or two people to transport easily, but not identical. If possible, the gravel pieces should be 2-3mm in diameter. The three best kinds of gravel to use are river gravel, granite chips, or marble chips. Avoid sea gravel as the shape is too uniform. Stick to one shade only. Plastic sheets are used to prevent the gravel from mixing with the soil, to stop the growth of weeds and to retain moisture

The shape and raking pattern of this dry garden suggest water in motion

Materials:
5 pieces natural rock.
10 x 30kg bags of gravel (tiny stone chips)
Plastic sheets to cover area of garden
Moss or similar groundcover
Pieces of granite or stone sufficient to edge three sides of your 3 x 2m area (i.e. approx. 7m); the pieces should be 10cm wide and any length
Cement and sand mixture (either bought ready mixed or prepared in a ratio of 5:5 or 7:3, depending on type and quality)

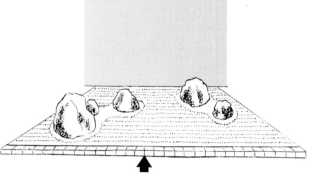

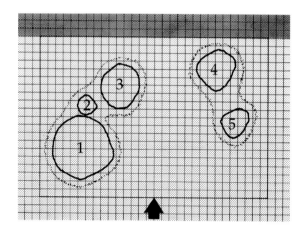

Construction

1. Level the land and remove all debris. If the soil is soft, pound with a heavy tool to create a firm base.

2. Mark out an area 3m by 2m then divide it into sections of one square meter.

3. Lay the plastic sheeting on the soil within the site. Place small rocks on it at intervals to secure it temporarily against the wind.

4. Arrange the rocks in two separate island groups. This is only a temporary setting, since you will have to remove them to make their foundations.

Group A: Stones 1,2,3 in diagram
Group B: Stones 4,5 in diagram
Since the shape of your stones will vary, this can only be a rough guide, and you should use your own judgment. Depending on the individual stone, it may be necessary to dig a foundation to bury a portion of the base and to lay cement for added stability. Use a knife to make holes in the sheets where the display stones will be positioned.

5. It is important to stand back and study the stone arrangement from a distance. When you are satisfied with the view, remove the stones to a separate area of the garden.

6. If necessary, lay the cement and sand mixture beneath where the stones are to be placed. Their shape will determine whether they need to be cemented into place.

7. Lay the stones in the correct position.

8. Place soil around the stones. The soil should frame the stone and be about 10cm higher than ground level.

9. Lay moss or other groundcover between the stones.

10. Lay the gravel on top of the plastic sheets to a depth of 4-6cm.

11. Lay the cement and sand mixture along the side of the garden not bordered by wall or fence. Lay the granite or pieces of stone into this.

12. Rake the gravel into a pattern, creating straight lines from left to right, then right to left in a zigzag

fashion. Always pull the rake behind you, never push it in front. When you have completed the straight lines, you can rake circles around the stones (see below for different raking patterns). This creates the sense of waves gently lapping against the shore.

13. Water the garden thoroughly with a sprinkler.

Raking the gravel into a pattern

6 | MAINTENANCE

Once your garden is complete, maintenance is extremely important. Otherwise, within a few months, all of your hard work and money will be lost.

This applies especially to plants, which require periodic trimming and careful weeding. If this is not done regularly, the garden will soon be reclaimed by nature and become wild.

The inanimate objects do not need such regular upkeep but should be checked for rot and color change. Indeed, the older and more weathered they become, the more authentic the garden appears. However, if for instance your bamboo fence is becoming a bit unstable, and there is a chance that a strong wind might cause it to collapse, it should be replaced.

PLANTS

Pine Trees

Pines like dry, sandy soil and should be planted or transplanted in the spring. As the branches bend easily without breaking they are easy to trim and tie into shape. A pine should not be trimmed before it reaches five years of age, with the ideal age for trimming being seven years. I would suggest that you purchase a specimen of five years and let it become established in your garden for two years before you start trimming.

I recommend that you use the Japanese black pine (*kuromatsu*). This is one of the most popular and hardiest of pines, and the variety that I usually use in gardens I have designed. It prefers a warmer climate and is extremely strong and resilient, flourishing in many different environments from polluted conditions to coastal regions with very strong winds.

A pond surrounded by a rock and flower garden and a traditional Japanese house. Maintenance costs for a private garden such as this one can be extremely high

There are two styles into which the pine is shaped: upright and twisting. The choice will depend on the trees' balance with the rest of the garden. Once the basic shape has been achieved you should only trim twice a year, in spring and fall. In the spring, the new buds should be pinched off, and in the fall the old and dead growth should be removed.

Bamboo

Bamboo is easy to maintain, inexpensive and is found in many different situations and climates. There are two important points to remember. Firstly, before the bamboo is established it will require a lot of water and high humidity. You may have to water it daily during the early stages but once established, it grows fast and spreads rapidly. The root growth is horizontal. When the bamboo reaches the required size you should make some kind of border to stop it from spreading.

Trimming is very easy and is done only once a year. In the first year you should ensure that your bamboo has a good water supply and by the following spring, providing it likes the situation, there should be a good growth of new bamboo shoots. Wait until the leaves appear on the new shoots before you begin trimming to the required height.

Each stem has side branches which grow from the individual sections. Leave three or four of these branched sections and remove the rest. Always trim slightly above the section you wish to retain. This is only carried out once a year, and in between the only maintenance it requires is regular watering.

Sometimes, quite unexpectedly, the bamboo will flower. This flowering stem should be cut off at ground level. Unfortunately, this heralds the death of the bamboo plant.

Moss

Moss is a very useful and effective means of ground cover. It is difficult to cultivate and requires constant high humidity but if you should be fortunate enough to have the ideal conditions, try and cultivate this beautiful plant. It will add a sense of age and maturity to your garden.

If moss will not grow in your environment, there are some alpine plants available which are good substitutes and can provide a similar effect. Japanese gardens are not usually level but contain hills, rocks and plant material and are therefore difficult to trim by machine. I would therefore suggest that you choose as your moss substitute a low and slow-growing plant variety since it will have to be cut by hand.

Moss is used not only as a ground cover, but as a complement to natural stone, stone lanterns, water basins and for waterfalls. If you should find some moss, lay it upon your stone or garden ornaments and keep it constantly moist. It may establish itself and is well worth the effort.

Weeding

Always remove weeds as soon as you notice them. Do not leave them until the next day; they are usually stronger than the plants and can soon kill them.

Dry gardens should not suffer from weeds, since weeds will not grow through the plastic sheeting.

Trimming

After several years, when you feel the plants have reached a sufficient height and size, you should start to control their growth through trimming. If possible, first read some books on the subject of trimming and try to practice the techniques in the garden for the first year and wait and see what the results are. You can always adapt and seek alternatives.

It is especially important to trim new buds, otherwise the shape of the plant will rapidly change.

If you leave trimming for too long, it may be too late to recreate the shape.

Above all, remember that you are dealing with nature. Take things slowly, be patient and follow the seasons. You will have many years to appreciate, practice and learn from your garden.

Replacing
Within two to three years, some of the plants may have died and will need to be replaced. Others will have become irreparably overgrown and should also be replaced. It is important not only to look at the individual plants but also at the relationship and balance with the rest of the garden when replacing them.

Fertilizing
Fertilize the plants at least once a year but not too often, either in early spring or early fall. Check for signs of disease or insects and apply any necessary remedies.

Groundcover
It is necessary to water the moss or other groundcover regularly until it is well established. Once established, you will need to trim some types regularly to keep them from growing too tall. Ground cover can also be a useful tool to prevent the growth of weeds.

ORNAMENTS

Bamboo fence
Bamboo is stronger than wood and does not rot or crack as quickly. It usually lasts between five and seven years. However, the part of the supporting rustic poles that is beneath the soil often rots. To check, you should shake the fence gently from time to time to see how much it moves. If there is a lot of movement, you should replace the rustic pole supports.

After several years, bamboo loses its natural oils and becomes a dull gray color. If this displeases you, you can paint it a natural bamboo color.

The *shuronawa* rope should last at least three to five years. The color will fade over time to a gray. If you dislike the resulting color, you can replace the string.

A low bamboo fence is used to divide two sections of this garden

Stepping Stones
Stone is one of the most durable, unchanging elements in the garden. However, if stepping stones are made of a sandy stone or are quite thin, after several years' use they may crack. You should then replace them with stone of a similar type and color.

Rocks of different styles and colors create an interesting effect in this path of stepping stones

Stone Lantern

In Japan, stone lanterns which look old are highly prized, because they epitomize the quality of *wabi*. You can age your lantern in two ways. Either pour water over the lantern as often as possible to create humidity in the stone so that it attracts moss, or paint the lantern with yoghurt to encourage mold.

The only danger that may threaten your stone ornaments is that the soil beneath them may sink, causing them to lean precariously. This may result from the weight of the lantern, the root growth of nearby plants, or from strong winds. If this happens, move the object, level the soil, then put it back in place.

A composition of a stone lantern, a stone water basin and a water pipe. A Buddha image is carved on the front of the water basin

GRAVEL

Gravel does not need to be raked very often; only when cleaning or weeding have disturbed the pattern. However, it should be kept clear of leaves and other debris, since they tend to stand out, particularly against the light gravel. Pets walking across the garden or fouling it may be another problem.

You can change the design of the raked gravel to create a different atmosphere, from a feeling of calm tranquillity to a more energetic pattern. For different raking patterns, see page 101.

After several years, the level of the gravel will sink, and you may need to add more. If so, take care to mix the old weathered gravel well with the new. Do not just lay the new on top, as the colors will vary.

Indoor dry garden. Care should be taken to keep it clear of leaves and other debris

WATER

After several years, there is the possibility that a pond, water basin or bamboo pipe may crack. To prevent this, check the water level from time to time, and if there is a sudden drop, locate the leak and either repair or replace the leaking part

If you have a water pump which is not in use during cold winter months, remove it and put it somewhere warm and dry. This is especially important if the pump is under water as, if the water freezes, it can do a great deal of damage.

ELECTRICAL CABLES

Electrical cables beneath the soil should be checked every two to three years. They risk damage by the heavy use of a garden tool. Check junction boxes and electrical connections to see if they are leaking water. If you find any leaks, repair or replace the relevant part immediately.

APPENDIX 1

When to plant
The correct season for planting varies according to
different environments and climates, but the information I have listed below can be taken as the
seasonal average.

Evergreen pine: plant between October and April
(the cold season).

Wide-leafed evergreen: plant between March and
November except when there is a lot of new shoot
growth (about May) or during a very hot season.

Deciduous wide-leafed trees and shrubs: plant
between November and March, after the leaves
fall but before new shoot or leaf growth.

Bamboo or palms: plant between April and
September, i.e., when the weather is warm, but
not during the hottest months.

There are two different ways of planting your
material: either straight or at an angle. Material is
often planted at an angle to create a feeling of
imbalance and an interesting asymmetrical effect.

Above: Tree trunks are purposely bent to create a feeling of asymmetry
Center: Asymmetrical shapes are created to add an interesting effect to the garden
Below: Some of the pine trees in this garden have been shaped so that their
branches almost touch the water

CHART OF RECOMMENDED PLANTS

a. Common Name
b. Japanese Name
c. Botanical Name
d. Specific Notes

Ground Cover Plants under 30 cm

1.
a. Liriope
b. *Yaburan*
c. *Liriope muscari*
d. Ground cover/ Green foliage/ Acid soils

Any dry site, in sun or light shade. Needs good drainage, but light soils that are very alkaline are not suitable.

2.
a. Day Lily
b. *Kanzō*
c. *Hemerocallisspp*
d. Ground cover/ Green foliage/ Damp clay and wet soil

After planting, if left undisturbed, sheaves of arching foliage will form large, weed-proof clumps. Each flower lasts for only one day.

3.
a. Fern, Common Polypody
b. *Shida*
c. *Polypodium vulgare*
d. Ground cover/ Green foliage/ Chalk soils
Stays green throughout winter. As a groundcover, provides a most effective carpet for dry soils. May also be planted on old tree stumps or in crevices in walls.

4.
a. Vinca, Lesser Periwinkle
b. *Nichinichisō*
c. *Vinca minor*
d. Ground cover/ Chalk soils

Like larger species, will tolerate dense shade and dryness, although prefers sun and well drained soil. Can also be planted in containers.

5.
a. Sasa
b. *Sasa*
c. *Sasa veitchii*
d. Ground cover/ Variegated leaves

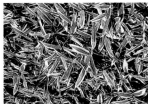

A short bamboo. Low and thicket-forming. Has interesting colors throughout winter. Can be planted in containers.

6.
a. Hosta
b. *Gibōshi*
c. *Hosta spp*
d. Ground cover/ Variegated leaves

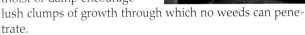

Rich soils that are either moist or damp encourage lush clumps of growth through which no weeds can penetrate.

7.
a. Solomon's Seal
b. *Amadokoro*
c. *Polygonatum odoratum*
d. Ground cover

Elegant. Grown mainly for green and cream foliage, though small bell-shaped flowers along leaf stalks have a special grace in spring. Moisture-retentive soil gives the best results.

8.
a. Fringed Iris
b. *Shaga*
c. *Iris japonica Thunb*
d. Ground cover
Grows from a mass of grassy
evergreen leaves. Flowers
best in shady spots. Flattish,
pale-lilac flowers are reminiscent of orchids.

9.
a. Moss
b. *Sugigoke*
c. *Polytrichum formosum Hedw*
d. Ground cover
Grows best where it receives
morning and late afternoon
sunlight, or in filtered shade.
Some varieties thrive in full sun, greening up during rainy
weather before it becomes dry and warm. If dried out,
revives when dampened.

Small Shrubs under 1 m

10.
a. Japanese yew
b. *Kyaraboku*
c. *Taxus cuspidata Sieb. et Zucc*
d. Small shrub
Short bushy leaves, curved or
straight, are dark green above and
golden-green below seed-cup.
Male and female flowers on
separate trees. Very hardy.
Has prolific side branches which
intermingle, so ideal for use as a natural style fence.

11.
a. Creeping Juniper
b. *Haibyakushin*
c. *Juniperus spp.*
d. Small shrub/ Ground cover
Wide-spreading conifer, so
excellent groundcover; long
branches densely set with
steely blue-green needles.Thrives in any well drained soil.

12.
a. Skimmia
b. *Miyamashikimi*
c. *Skimmia japonica*
d. Small shrub/ Ground cover
Rounded shrub; bears splen-
did red berries which are
exceptionally long-lasting.
Likes moist, rather acid loams and partially shaded positions. Male forms produce the most attractive flowers.

13.
a. Aucuba
b. *Aoki*
c. *Aucuba japonica Thunb*
d. Small shrub/ Chalk, clay/
Dry shade/ Seaside
Surprisingly attractive, even in
deep shade. At its best, deli-
cately toothed leaves provide a deep and shiny background for brightred berries which appear when male and
female plants are grown together.

14.
a. Azalea
b. *Tsutsuji*
c. *Rhododendron spp.*
d. Small shrub/ Ground
cover/ Acid soils/ Fall foliage
Can be used to form patches
of groundcover. In winter,
remaining leaves take on attractive coppery tints. A partially shaded site preserves the brilliant flower color and
lessens the likelihood of frost.

15.
a. Pieris
b. *Asebi*
c. *Pieris japonica*
d. Small shrub/ Ground
cover/ Acid soils
Slow-growing shrub; prefers
a sheltered site, as variegated
leaves and hanging bunches of flowers are easily be damaged by frost and wind. Young leaves are lightly tinged
pink.

16.
a. Forsythia
b. *Rengyō*
c. *Forsythia suspensa*
d. Small shrub/ Climber/
Chalk soils
Easy to grow in any soil,
including heavy clay. Looks

especially nice fan-trained against a wall or sprawling over
a fence or low bank. Its ability to flower quite well in full
shade makes it a useful wall covering.

17.
a. Bridal Wreath
b. *Yukiyanagi*
c. *Spiraea arguta*
d. Small shrub/ Mass of flowers
Rounded shrub; in spring,
each curved stem is covered

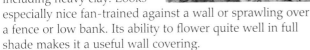

with numerous, tightly packed flowers. Masses of blossom
and shape make this a spectacular plant during its flowering season.

18.
a. Japanese Quince
b. *Boke*
c. *Chaenomeles lagenaria*
d. Small shrub/ Clay soils/
Fruit bearing
Very hardy. Suitable for any
soil. Does well on cold, sun-
less walls. Edible fruit ripens in late summer and early fall.

Large Shrubs and Trees under 2 m

19.
a. Castor Oil Plant
b. *Yatsude*
c. *Fatsia Japonica*
d. Large shrub/ Dense shade/
Green foliage
Sparsely branched shrub
noted for big, handsome

leaves. Will grow in dense shade. In cold regions, may
require a warm, sheltered position.

20.
a. Camellia
b. *Tsubaki*
c. *Camellia japonica*
d. Large shrub/ Green
foliage/ Acid-soil
Winter-flowering plant.

Needs a moist, peaty soil and,
in cold districts, enough warmth to produce plenty of
buds.

21.
a. Chamaecyparis
b. *Chabohiba*
c. *Chamaecyparis obtusa*
d. Large shrub/ Aromatic
leaves
Slow-growing, but curva-
ceous sprays of dark green

leaves can be appreciated from the
very earliest stages of this conifer's life.
Grows poorly in dry and alkaline conditions.

22.
a. Bamboo
b. *Take*
c. *Phyllostachys nigra*
d. Large shrub/ Green foliage
Requires moisture, shelter
and sunshine. As plant
matures, canes change from a

soft green color to yellow marked with purple.

23.
a. Maple
b. *Momiji*
c. *Acer Palmatum*
d. Large shrub/ Acid-soil/ Autumn foliage
Most attractive plant forms a spreading heap of feathery leaves. Grows best in a moist soil that is acidic or neutral. Shelter from cold winds and early morning frost.

24.
a. Heavenly bamboo
b. *Nanten*
c. *Nandina domestica*
d. Large shrub/ Aromatic leaves
Slow-growing, stiff cane. Flushes red in spring and purplish red in fall. Small white flowers in mid-summer come on erect stalked panicles.

25.
a. Spindle Tree
b. *Nishikigi*
c. *Euonymus alatus*
d. Large shrub/ Autumn foliage/ Chalk soils/ Bark/ Twigs
Chief attraction is bright pinkish scarlet leaves in fall. Stiff spreading branches have corky 1/2 cm wide flat wings attached to them.

26.
a. Chinese Witch Hazel
b. *Mansaku*
c. *Hamamelis mollis*
d. Large shrub/ Acid-soil/ Fragrant flowers
Robus and very sweetly scented flowers appear in large numbers on the naked twigs and branches of this outstanding winter-flowering plant. Acid soils that are well drained. In fall, leaves turn yellow.

27.
a. Rose of Sharon
b. *Mukuge*
c. *Hibiscus syriacus*
d. Large shrub/ Acid-soil
Best in well-drained soils, including chalky ones. Must have a warm and sheltered site if flowers are to appear in sizeable quantities and not to be damaged by early frosts.

Large Trees over 2 m

28.
a. Japanese Black Pine
b. *Kuromatsu*
c. *Pinus thunbergii Parl*
d. Large tree/ Protection against wind
Projecting, twisted branches form an irregular crown. Entire tree often leans when mature. Long intercepting branches when old. For use in Japanese garden, bend or twist branches to required shape and use as a focal point.

29.
a. Japanese red pine
b. *Akamatsu*
c. *Pinus densiflora Sieb. et zucc Large tree*
d. Dry soil/ Unpolluted air

Shape is often twisted or crooked. Broad and irregular-ly-shaped conical paired needles of medium length, are bright green and sharply pointed. Grows throughout Japan.

30.
a. Chinese Juniper
b. *Ibuki*
c. *Juniperus chinensis L*
d. Large tree/ Unpolluted air

Young leaves are prickly, dark green. Grows well in windy and polluted conditions. From ancient times planted in temples & parks in Japan. Very strong growing; can be planted anywhere. Prolific side branches make this an ideal plant to grow as a fence, as they intermingle and join with each other.

31.
a. Japanese umbrella pine
b. *Kōyamaki*
c. *Sciadopitys verticillata Sieb. et Zucc*
d. Large tree/ Moist soil/ Unpolluted air

Broad conical shape, with irregular, narrowly conical leaves of medium length arranged in characteristic united pairs. Leaves are glossy green above and yellow-green beneath, arranged in whorls. Straight growth, noble appearance.

32.
a. Maidenhair Tree
b. *Ichō*
c. *Ginkgo bilobal*
d. Large tree/ Deciduous tree

Varies from narrow and upright to broadly spreading. Grows slowly. Thick yellow male flowers are rare; female flowers are single or paired, pale yellow. Plant young trees, preferably in groups, and trim regularly.

33.
a. Cherry
b. *Sakura*
c. *Prunus spp*
d. Large tree/ Lime and chalk soils

Big group of deciduous trees. Leaves are simple, and often fragrant when crushed. Flowers five-petalled, white or pink; in doubled forms, number of petals is increased. Sun-loving. Usually very hardy.

34.
a. Magnolia
b. *Mokuren*
c. *Magnolia spp*
d. Large tree/ Full sun

Deciduous or evergreen. Big simple leaves. Bares single bisexual flowers; cone-like fruit, red or pink. Does not thrive in chalk soil. Pruning unnecessary.

35.
a. Willow
b. *Yanagi*
c. *Salix spp*
d. Large tree/ Full sun/ Very hardy
Deciduous. Leaves are simple, usually alternate between long and narrow, and shaped like pointed teeth. Usually have either male or female flowers, both of which grow without petals in silken hairy catkins. Tolerant of moisture. Fast-growing.

36.
a. Crape myrtle
b. *Sarusuberi*
c. *Lagerstroemia indica L.*
d. Large tree/ Ornamental tree
Deciduous, grows up to 6 m. Smooth mottled grey bark,

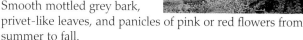

privet-like leaves, and panicles of pink or red flowers from summer to fall.

Climbing Plants

37.
a. Wisteria
b. *Fuji*
c. *Wisteria sinensis*
d. Climbing plant/ Rich, moist soil
Deciduous; flowers from spring to summer. Flowers

violet-blue to white. Requires normal pruning and some shelter to protect flower buds from frost damage.

38.
a. Morning glory
b. *Asagao*
c. *Ipomea rubro-caerulea*
d. Climbing plant/ Fertile soil
The beautiful sky-blue of this twining climber is the color most often associated with the morning glory. Will not grow without warmth and shelter.

39.
a. Trumpet creeper
b. *Nōsenkazura*
c. *Campsis chinensis Voss.*
d. Climbing plant/ Warm site
All species and forms require a very warm site to become established fairly quickly and to flower. Stems have aerial roots which will cling to walls.

40.
a. Clematis
b. *Tessen*
c. *Clematis spp*
d. Climbing plant/ Ornamental flower
Needs a rich, preferably alkaline, soil. Roots require shading from direct sunlight, and twining leaf-stalks need support.

41.
a. Honeysuckle
b. *Nindō*
c. *Lonicera japonica halliana*
d. Climbing plant/ Fragrant in evening
Very vigorous; can easily cover an unsightly shed with its slender, twining stems. Also makes a good groundcover.

Flowers

42.
a. Lily
b. *Yuri*
c. *Lilium speciosum rubrum*
d. Flower/ Cut flower
Requires a warm, sheltered position with free draining acid soil. Flowers from summer to autumn. Flower color deep pink; height;1.5m.

43.
a. Crocosmia
b. *Kinpōge*
c. *Crocosmia curtonus
Lucifer NA*
d. Flower/ Ornamental leaves
Brilliantly colored flowers
appear in early or mid- summer. Needs a sheltered site in
colder areas. Good drainage
gives particularly satisfactory
results.

44.
a. Peony
b. *Botan*
c. *Paeonia suffruticosa*
d. Flower/ Ornamental leaves
An ancient plant from China.
To produce massive, heavy, fragrant
flowers, needs deep rich soil, gener-
ous mulching, and plenty of moisture in the growing season after
flowering. Likes cold winters, during
which will become dormant.

45.
a. Bellflower
b. *Kikyō*
c. *Platycoden grandiflorum*
d. Flower
Native to China and Japan.
Perennial plant to 45 cm.
Blue, 4-5 cm saucer-shaped
flowers all summer. Cultivars include double, white flow-
ered forms in which the flowers retain the balloon shape
of the buds.

46.
a. Chrysanthemum
b. *Kiku*
c. *Chrysanthemum spp.*
d. Flower
Likes fertile, preferably alkaline, soils. Good drainage
prolongs its life. More and
more varieties of chrysanthemums
are being produced in a wide range
of colors.

47.
a. Iris
b. *Kakitsubata*
c. *Iris laevigata*
d. Flower
Prefers to be grown in shallow
water, but will do almost equally
well in very moist soil. Softly colored
foliage and mellow blue flowers
make a particulary attractive combination.

APPENDIX 2

UNITED KINGDOM

Kyoto Garden, Holland Park, London W8, England

Opened in September 1991, this is London's first authentic public Japanese garden and was built to commemorate the 1991 Japan Festival. It is on the site of a garden which was made in the 1890s for the fifth Lord Ilchester and his wife. The new garden was constructed by ten gardeners who came especially from Japan. The rocks for the waterfall and stream and the plants are from the United Kingdom.

Heale House, Woodford, Salisbury, Wiltshire, England

The stream for this garden is fed by water from the River Avon. At its heart is a Japanese teahouse, now in fragile condition, which was brought back from Japan in 1901 by the Honorable Louis Greville, great-uncle of the present owner.

Tatton Park Japanese Garden, The Tatton Estate, Knutsford, Cheshire, England
In 1910 the third Lord Egerton employed Japanese gardeners to landscape the garden. The water flowing into the pond, stream and waterfall, combined with the maples and evergreens, creates a very tranquil atmosphere. A special feature of the garden is a lake with an island, on which is a Shintō shrine which was brought from Japan.

Cottered Japanese Garden, Cottered, Hertfordshire, England
In 1905, Mr. Herbert Goode visited Japan and became fascinated by Japanese gardens. He transformed six acres of his property into a Japanese garden, moving tons of earth to create miniature mountains, islands and ponds. Some of the trees were brought from Japan. In 1923 with the help of Mr. Seyemon Kusumoto he added bridges and a two-story Japanese house. The garden was called *Kōrakuen* meaning the garden of good luck and long life.

Rivington Terraced Gardens, Lever Park, Rivington, Lancashire, England
The garden was created in 1922 by the landscape architect, T. H. Mawson. It contained teahouses, lanterns, pagodas, bridges, miniature waterfalls and a one acre lake. From 1925 onwards the garden fell into disrepair and was vandalized. It is now owned by the North West Water Authority and the terraced Japanese garden has been restored.

Compton Acres Garden, Canford Cliffs, Poole, Dorset, England

These famous private gardens are shady and sheltered and include woodland, semi-tropical, glen, rock, palm court and heather gardens. Besides the Japanese garden there are also Roman, English and Italian gardens. In 1950 the property was purchased by Mr. J.S. Beard, J.P., who restored and opened the gardens to the public. A Japanese architect and workmen brought everything to England from Japan and the garden is reputed to be the only completely genuine Japanese garden in Europe. The trees and plants are mostly Japanese varieties.

Enniskerry Garden, Powerscourt, Enniskerry, County Wicklow, Ireland
Although this is not an authentic garden it has great charm and is very peaceful. It was built around 1910 and the design is based upon the theme of life. Amongst the features are two paths which meet at the "Marriage Bridge" and a grotto which contains a grave. There is also a bridge, pagoda and a pond.

The National Stud Japanese Garden, Tully Kildare, Ireland
Lord Wavertree's garden was made by the Japanese gardener Eida and his son Minoru between 1906 and 1910. The garden was planned to symbolize the human life cycle and includes such features as the Cave of Birth, the Marriage Bridge, the Hill of Ambition, the Chair of Old Age and the Gateway to Eternity.

Duthie Park, Aberdeen, Scotland

The Japanese Garden here was designed by the author of this book and dedicated in June 1987 to commemorate the fortieth anniversary of the atomic bombing of Hiroshima in 1945. It is a token of sympathy from the City of Aberdeen. Inspired by the idea of peace, a stream flows into a pond designed in the shape of the Chinese character for the word "heart" (*kokoro*). There are many evergreen Japanese plants and the maples, cherries, camellias and azaleas provide touches of seasonal color.

Dollar Japanese Garden, Cowden Castle, Dollar, Muckhart Churchyard, Muckhart, Scotland
This garden was the creation of the rich and eccentric Miss Christie. In 1906 she visited Japan and engaged the services of Taki Honda, a lady graduate from the Imperial School of Garden Design who arrived in Scotland in 1907. In 1925 Professor Suzuki, an advisor to Kew Gardens in England, found a Japanese gardener to work full time for Miss Christie; he was known only as Matsuo and was to spend the rest of his life at Cowden.

The Tea Garden, Gateshead, Durham, England

This garden was created as part of the National Garden Festival in 1990. The designer and gardeners were brought especially from Japan, as were many of the materials including the teahouse and the garden ornaments. The garden includes many different types of British gardens, as well as examples from other countries.

FRANCE
Japanese Garden, Jardin Albert Kahn,
Boulogne-Billancourt

The garden was created by the German-born Mr. Albert Kahn and is situated in a suburb of Paris. It was made in the early part of the twentieth century by a designer and gardeners from Japan. The original teahouse and garden was restored about twenty years ago. There is a recent addition of an avant-garde Japanese garden designed by a French landscape architect.

Claude Monet Museum, Giverny 27620, Gasny

Claude Monet's property at Giverny was left to the Academie des Beaux-Arts in 1966 by his son. After the completion of large-scale restoration work in

1980, it was inaugurated as the Claude Monet Museum. The gardens have been replanted as they once were. The Japanese water garden, with its famous Japanese bridge, water lilies and pond, is formed by a tributary of the River Epte. It lies at the far end of the garden, shaded by weeping willows. This scene was the inspiration for what is considered to be one of Monet's masterpieces.

GERMANY
Innengarten des Museums, Museum fur Ostasiatische Kunst, Cologne
Architect: Mr. M. Nagara

UNITED STATES OF AMERICA
Tenshin-en, Museum of Fine Arts, Boston, Massachussetts

Tenshin-en (Garden of the Heart of Heaven) was dedicated on October 24th 1988 and is named in honor of one of the first curators of the Department of Asiatic Art, Ikakura Kakuzo (1906-1913). The garden is an important addition to the Museum's world-renowned Asiatic collection. Designed by Kinsaku Nakane of Kyoto, Japan, it is a contemplative viewing garden in the *karesansui* style, harking back to the Zen temple gardens of 15th-century Japan.

Japanese Tea Garden, Golden Gate Park, San Francisco, California
This is an extensive Japanese garden dating from an international exposition.

Duke Gardens, Somerville, New Jersey
There are acres of gardens in glasshouses, including a Japanese garden.

Hillwood Museum Gardens, 4155 Linnean Avenue N.W., Washington D.C.
This is a Japanese garden within the extensive estate of the late Marjorie Merrwerth.

The Morikawa Yamato Colony, Palm Beach County, Florida
This is both a Japanese garden and a museum.

Oriental Stroll Garden, Hammond Museum, North Salem, New York

Seiwa-En, Missouri Botanical Garden, St. Louis, Missouri

Tennessee Japanese Garden, Tennessee Botanical Garden and Fine Arts Centre, Cheekwood, Nashville, Tennessee

ISRAEL
Tikotin Museum of Japanese Art, Haifa, Israel
Japanese garden of the Hefsiba-Kibbutz, Hefsiba

INDEX